TO

_____

FROM

_____

DATE

_____

100 Days of Faith over Fear: A Devotional Journal
Copyright 2019, Lisa Stilwell
First Edition, August 2019

Published by:

P.O. Box 1010
Siloam Springs, AR 72761
dayspring.com

Cover Design by Brady Voss
Typeset by Jason D. Kingsley
Printed in China
Prime: 89890
ISBN: 978-1-68408-618-4

Foreword by Pastor and Bestselling Author ROBERT J. MORGAN

100 DAYS OF

FAITH

— OVER —

FEAR

DEVOTIONAL JOURNAL

LISA STILWELL

FOREWORD

Oh, the many faces of fear we meet! And each leaves a lasting mark on our hearts. One of my earliest recollections is hiding behind a boxwood as my mother was wheeled out of the house on a stretcher and placed in an ambulance. I don't recall my age—perhaps four or so. And I remember nothing else about the incident, nor do I now know what was wrong with her—I think it turned out to be a slipped disk. But that single moment left an early and indelible groove on the copper plates of my memory. My subsequent six decades have added so many scratches, scars, and gouges to the copper plates that, apart from the grace of God, my mind would be a crisscrossed mess of anxieties, phobias, and distresses.

When dealing with fear, we have a lot of resources to turn to, such as physicians, friends, and counselors. We need them all, because overcoming stubborn fear requires determined effort. But our greatest help comes from the Great Physician, the Friend who never forsakes us, and the counsel of God's unfailing Word.

There is something about the promises and reassurances of Scripture that repairs and rejuvenates the mind and soul. I have a small desk by a window where my Bible stays open and where God's ear is never closed. During many a distressing season, I've gone there seeking His promises amid my problems and His fatherly comfort during the concerns and crises of life. The Lord cannot fail me and never will, and His Word has been a perpetual restorative to my troubled heart. And not to mine only.

I have a library of Christian biographies and autobiographies, and each of them is a testimony to God's grace amid the perils of life. We have a Helper who knows every threat we feel, and He is fearless in the face of them all. He turns curses into blessings, and weakness into strength. He wants us to know how little we have to fear when He is near. A thorough knowledge of Scripture provides a solid basis for faith, and growing faith results in lessening anxiety. We'll either wear ourselves down with fretting or we'll be lifted up on the eagle's wings of faith.

Lisa's book, *100 Days of Faith over Fear*, uncovers some of the Bible's best verses for choosing self-possession over the preoccupation of fear. Her insights and applications will strike chimes in your heart. In fact, I had a hard time wrestling this manuscript away from my wife, Katrina, who battles multiple sclerosis and who had the printed pages spread out before her. "This is excellent," Katrina said. "Hurry and give it back!"

So if you're hiding behind some boxwood today, read this book. It'll point you to God's Word, which will point you to God's Son; and the many faces of fear can never withstand the fearless face of our Lord Jesus Christ.

—ROBERT J. MORGAN

INTRODUCTION

Fear…It connotes a lifetime of struggle for almost everyone. No matter our age, race, financial status, or demographic, we all succumb to the power of fear to some degree. Chances are, since you are reading this, you live with fear to some degree as well.

There are many legitimate things to be afraid of—failure, abandonment, bullies, consequences. The list is endless. Sometimes, even if there isn't anything to be afraid of, we'll create something to fret about because the circle of fear is where we've lived for so long. Being unafraid is uncomfortable.

Then there's the constant battle from outside forces to divide our time, our energy, and our determination to combat our fears. When we are drained of the power we have for overcoming fear, we relent in our weakness and submit to it instead.

How do I know this? I lived in the bondage of fear for much of my life, but with God's help and healing, and learning the truth about who I am as His child, there came a time when I wanted out of that bondage—*for good*. God took a mostly frightened, insecure, uneducated young woman from thinking she couldn't do anything for Him (because she was too afraid) and paved her way up to a senior-level position in the Christian corporate world. The road wasn't easy—there were many battles to get through before realizing the power I possessed (the power we *all* possess as Christians) for overcoming fear, but victory ultimately won. This doesn't mean I'm free from the temptation to fear, but the fight of resistance has become shorter and stronger over time.

I want you to have victory over fear too. If even one more heart can experience freedom from the physical and emotional setbacks fear brings, angels will sing, and fellow believers can celebrate together to bring hope and inspire others to do the same.

This devotional journal is not meant to be *the* answer for helping rid you of fear, but hopefully it will help in your journey. The entries were written to both inspire and challenge you to really look at what form fear has taken in your life. (I have found it's often more than one.) They were also written to encourage and empower a stronghold of faith—in a God who sees and who cares immensely. Included are scriptures for meditation and memorizing, which help heal wounds, both old and new, and spur growth in the confidence that is ours when we walk in complete trust in the Savior.

While there may be many things to fear, there is only One to have real faith in, and He is here now to provide assurance, peace, and undying devotion that cannot be shaken. Each moment we can choose to either give in to fear or draw from the faith we hold within. Let us journey together not only to demolish fear but to feed our faith so there can be freedom, restoration, and renewed hope to live and to love the way God intended.

Father, I am ready—I am ready to start eliminating the things that keep me bound in fear and begin living in the freedom You have promised for my life. I call to You and trust You to be with me now to surround me, envelop me, and empower me to walk this journey with You.

FACE JESUS

You've probably heard and even said, "You've got to face your fears." After all, it makes sense to face something you're afraid of in order to overpower it. David faced Goliath before throwing the stone that killed him—but not before focusing on his almighty God (I Samuel 17). So often we think that facing something means focusing on it. But focusing on what you're afraid of only accomplishes one thing: it grows bigger. Instead of facing your fears, focus on Jesus. Look at Him and say, "My eyes are on You today, Lord. I'm walking into battle, but my eyes are on You." With God in your sights, you can overcome whatever Goliath you are facing.

When all the Israelite men saw Goliath, they retreated from him terrified....
David said to the Philistine..."I come against you in the name
of the LORD of Armies, the God of the ranks of Israel....
Today, the LORD will hand you over to me."

I SAMUEL 17:24, 45–46

We are powerless against this great multitude which is coming against us.
We do not know what to do, but our eyes are on You.

II CHRONICLES 20:12 AMP

I am able to do all things through him who strengthens me.

PHILIPPIANS 4:13

Let us run with endurance the race that lies before us,
keeping our eyes on Jesus, the source and perfecter of our faith.

HEBREWS 12:1-2

Lord, I am focusing on You today. I will rest in Your presence and see nothing but the truth of Your power within me. I will rest in knowing that You are my protector and shield, and that You are already fighting on my behalf today. I have nothing to fear.

HEARING IS NOT BELIEVING

Fear is a lie—that we believe. The lie itself isn't fear, it's merely a lie from the enemy planted in our heads to instill fear. And lies are powerless unless we believe them. Like the way a drug is just a pill until it's ingested. Once it's swallowed, the moisture and acids in the digestive system activate the release of its contents and carry its power to the bloodstream. It doesn't work until it's fed by the environment it needs.

The same is true about the promises in God's Word—they are promises on a page until we believe them. As soon as we do, the power they hold is released into our lives, and we can experience an indescribable peace that passes all understanding. We are constantly faced with what to believe, and what we believe is always a choice. Which will you choose?

[Satan]...does not stand in the truth, because there is no truth in him.
When he lies, he speaks out of his own character,
for he is a liar and the father of lies.

JOHN 8:44 ESV

You will know the truth, and the truth will set you free.

JOHN 8:32

Send Your light and Your truth; let them lead me. Let them bring me
to Your holy mountain, to Your dwelling place.

PSALM 43:3

*Everyone who hears these words of Mine and acts on them
will be like a wise man who built his house on the rock.*

MATTHEW 7:24

*Lord, I believe You. I believe the promises in Your Word for my own life. Help me
to see a lie for what it is and to send it away as fast as it comes. I want to soak
in Your truth and grow in the life it gives.*

FEAR, AN IDOL?

Have you ever stopped to think that fear can be an idol? One usually thinks of an idol as a famous movie star or singer who makes us feel good inside. But an idol is anything that receives more of your attention than God. And if you spend more hours thinking about what you're afraid of, fear indeed becomes an idol. You may not think, *I'm going to idolize my fears today*, but unless there is a conscious decision and determination to focus on God, fear will slither in and consume—even drive—your thoughts. So steer your attention toward God and His promises. Even if you have to redirect yourself over and over, keep herding your thoughts—toward His power, His goodness, and His faithfulness to you. Make Him the idol of your life.

Those who cherish worthless idols abandon their faithful love,
but as for me, I will sacrifice to You with a voice of thanksgiving.

JONAH 2:8-9

They worshiped their idols, which led to their downfall.

PSALM 106:36 NLT

I will meditate on Your precepts and think about Your ways.

PSALM 119:15

You shall have no other gods before Me.

EXODUS 20:3 NKJV

_____

_____

_____

_____

_____

_____

_____

_____

_____

_____

_____

_____

_____

_____

_____

_____

_____

Lord, I need Your help with my thoughts. Sometimes it's a minute-by-minute battle to stay focused on You instead of my fears. Help me, guard me against the temptation to look away from You—the One who holds my life and loves me more than any other.

TAKE HIM AT HIS WORD

Fear is unbelief, that is, not believing God. Put another way, fear contradicts God, so when we succumb to it, it's no wonder we're so miserable! Any state of mind or being that opposes God takes us out of the comfort of His graces and into anxiety-ridden, hellish existence. This is why, when we don't believe God and take Him at His Word, we become anxious, sick, discouraged, angry, panicked, and consumed with worry. Fear isn't particular about which of these symptoms we have, it just makes sure at least one, if not all, resides in us.

Let us follow Abraham's lead and believe God. Let us take Him at face value. Trust Him in *all* areas of life. Especially, let's believe *He is for us*. His love is real, and His Word is truth. We just have to believe.

Does God give you the Spirit and work miracles among you by your doing the works of the law? Or is it by believing what you heard—just like Abraham who believed God, and it was credited to him for righteousness? You know, then, that those who have faith, these are Abraham's sons.

GALATIANS 3:5–7

If some unbelieving outsiders walk in on a service where people are speaking out God's truth, the plain words will bring them up against the truth and probe their hearts. Before you know it, they're going to be on their faces before God, recognizing that God is among you.

I CORINTHIANS 14:25 THE MESSAGE

Abraham believed God, and it was credited
to him for righteousness.

ROMANS 4:3

Lord, I do believe—at certain times, when I'm completely focused on You, and after a prayer has been answered. I need help believing in the in-between times, when You seem silent or I get preoccupied. I love You and want the faith to believe all the time, just like Abraham.

THE FAITH LANE

If ever there were a track event we could all participate in, it'd be the heat between faith and fear. Each has its own lane in a daily race. Just as a race track has lines to keep competitors in their own lanes, so faith and fear remain opponents. One is dark and the other is light, and the two don't mix. No one can run in both lanes—we each must choose which one to occupy. At the end of the day, or lane, there can be crippling exhaustion, even growing fear. The other, a glowing view of Jesus with outstretched arms and His promise of peace. Which lane will you run in today?

Trust in the LORD with all your heart, and do not rely on your own understanding; in all your ways know him, and he will make your paths straight.

PROVERBS 3:5–6

How long will I store up anxious concerns within me, agony in my mind every day? How long will my enemy dominate me?

PSALM 13:2

Can any of you add one moment to his life span by worrying?

LUKE 12:25

Let us run with endurance the race that is set before us,
looking to Jesus, the founder and perfecter of our faith.

HEBREWS 12:1–2 ESV

_____
_____
_____
_____
_____
_____
_____
_____
_____
_____
_____
_____
_____
_____
_____
_____
_____
_____
_____

Lord, I want to run life in the faith lane. Help me to keep moving forward and remain focused on the belief that You care and are with me every step until I cross the finish line, right into Your arms.

CHOOSE LOVE

Fear is a choice. And since living in fear is a choice, why do so many of us opt for it? Why, oh why do we open the door of our hearts so quickly and let fear fly in? Is it because we try to resist it in our own feeble strength instead of God's power? Or perhaps it's because fear has become a comfortable place—it's what we've known for so long. Sometimes living in fear feels so normal, it's only natural not to change it. Or maybe it's because we aren't fully accepting of the vast amount of love God has for us. God's perfect love casts out fear, which happens when we truly believe that God loves us just the way we are.

He chose us to be His children. Let us choose Him—let us choose love. Let us welcome God's love wholeheartedly. Let fear dissolve, as it should, into the freedom that is ours through Christ and His care.

Where God's love is, there is no fear, because God's perfect love takes away fear. It is punishment that makes a person fear. So love is not made perfect in the person who has fear.

I JOHN 4:18 ICB

Guard your heart above all else, for it is the source of life.

PROVERBS 4:23

I have trusted in Your faithful love; my heart will rejoice in Your deliverance. I will sing to the LORD because He has treated me generously.

PSALM 13:5-6

He chose us in Him, before the foundation of the world,
to be holy and blameless in love before Him.

EPHESIANS 1:4

_____

_____

_____

_____

_____

_____

_____

_____

_____

_____

_____

_____

_____

_____

_____

_____

_____

_____

Father, thank You for choosing me, for calling me Your beloved child.
I love You, and I choose You today. Please cast out the fear that beckons my heart
and help me walk in the truth and freedom of Your love.

SMALL FAITH, BIG GOD

So often when we go through a difficulty that rings our fear bell, someone will say, "You just need more faith." Then we think, *Easy for you to say. You're not going through what I'm going through!* It's these times you might be tempted to compare your seeming lack of faith with someone else's over-abundance, only to feel even worse. But be careful not to compare. The disciples struggled with faith, even after they witnessed Jesus' miracles firsthand! What matters is staying focused on the God who loves you and is with you. He is for you and will help you. Keep calling His name and believing in the power you have through even a mustard-seed-like faith in Jesus. It is real, and it is yours for the asking.

———

[Jesus] said to [the disciples], "Where is your faith?"
They were fearful and amazed, asking one another,
"Who then is this? He commands even the winds
and the waves, and they obey Him!"

LUKE 8:25

Jesus said, "You of little faith,
why are you discussing among yourselves
that you do not have bread?"

MATTHEW 16:8

This I know: God is for me.

PSALM 56:9

Truly I tell you, if you have faith the size of a mustard seed...
nothing will be impossible for you.

MATTHEW 17:20

_____
_____
_____
_____
_____
_____
_____
_____
_____
_____
_____
_____
_____
_____
_____
_____
_____

Father, my level of faith seems so weak and small compared to the mountain of trouble that weighs on my heart. Yet I'm comforted to know that even minute faith can transform an impossible situation into a miraculous one. I'm so grateful and glad I serve a mighty God.

CONTROLLING OUR THOUGHTS

Fear takes all of us on mental journeys where "what if," "can't," and "won't" become instant traveling lie companions. ***What if** I don't get the job?...I **can't** do anything right...I'm afraid I **won't** make it...*It's very hard to make the lies go away. They don't leave on request or even on command when we try to silence them in our own power. But when we quote Scripture, we are able to demolish these arguments and take every thought captive to *Him*. They must go away when God's Word enters in. **"What** father among you, **if** his son asks for a fish, will give him a snake...?"** (Luke 11:11). **"I can** do all things through Christ who strengthens me"** (Philippians 4:13 NKJV). **"I will** bless the LORD who counsels me—even at night when my thoughts trouble me"** (Psalm 16:7, emphasis added).

Taking every thought captive to Christ is the surest way to keep our minds filled with faith and belief in His loving care.

Send your light and your truth; let them lead me.
Let them bring me to your holy mountain, to your dwelling place.
Then I will come to the altar of God, to God, my greatest joy.
I will praise you with the lyre, God, my God.

PSALM 43:3–4

Therefore, I [Paul] say this and testify in the Lord:
You should no longer live as the Gentiles live,
in the futility of their thoughts. They are darkened
in their understanding, excluded from the life of God.

EPHESIANS 4:17–18

*Casting down the imaginations, and every high thing
that is exalted against the knowledge of God, and bringing
into captivity every thought to the obedience of Christ.*

II CORINTHIANS 10:5 GNV

_____

_____

_____

_____

_____

_____

_____

_____

_____

_____

_____

_____

_____

_____

_____

_____

*Lord, the next time lies start to fill my mind, please help me to stop and speak
Your words of power and truth to demolish them. Help me to take every thought
captive to Your promises and truly believe them for myself.*

FEAR-FILLED OR TRUST-FILLED?

We all look to sources we trust for meeting our needs. And if we are honest, we usually start with ourselves...then our families or our pastors. We know in theory that God is the one true Source of provision, but we still struggle to apply that truth deep within us on a daily basis—to really walk in confidence because we are fully abiding in *His* care. Is this because we have been disappointed or don't like His answers to past prayers? Or maybe we simply don't understand Him or we don't know Him well (it's impossible to trust someone we don't know). Bottom line is, when we don't trust God, we are basically telling Him we think we know better, and that's a fear-filled frame of mind to be in...because we don't know better. Trusting God is the safest, calmest, warmest, loveliest place to be. The promises in His Word are truth for the soul. What do you need to trust Him with today?

Trust in the LORD with all your heart,
and do not rely on your own understanding;
in all your ways know Him,
and He will make your paths straight.

PROVERBS 3:5–6

The LORD is my strength and my shield;
my heart trusts in Him, and I am helped.

PSALM 28:7

Jesus never insisted that His followers understand Him.
He insisted that they trust Him.

—CHRIS TIEGREEN

The precepts of the LORD are right, making the heart glad;
the command of the LORD is radiant, making the eyes light up.

PSALM 19:8

_____

_____

_____

_____

_____

_____

_____

_____

_____

_____

_____

_____

_____

_____

_____

_____

_____

Lord, please forgive me for ever thinking I know what's best for me more than You do. I confess, it's a daily struggle. Please help to trust You more. You have never failed me in the past; forgive me for not trusting You with my future.

FEAR OF THE FUTURE

If you're like most people, the minute you start thinking about the future and upcoming needs, you begin to worry. Will you graduate? Will you get the job? Will you ever get well? Will you accomplish retirement goals and live out your dreams? It's enough to raise your blood pressure and make your eye twitch. That good night's sleep you wanted? Gone. These are times when God leans down and whispers, "Dear one, you've moved from your role as worshiper and stepped into My role as provider...."

We were not meant to carry the future—it's a weight only God can bear. We were made to glorify Him through our daily living and worship—right where we are today. In the process, He promises to provide...one day at a time. The future is not ours to figure out, nor are the answers to our needs. Let's leave that role in its rightful place.

Therefore I tell you: Don't worry about your life.

MATTHEW 6:25

*He causes grass to grow for the livestock and provides crops
for man to cultivate, producing food from the earth...
and bread that sustains human hearts.*

PSALM 104:14–15

*The LORD will continually lead you;
He will feed you even in parched regions....
You will be like a well-watered garden,
like a spring that continually produces water.*

ISAIAH 58:11 NET

Your heavenly Father knows that you need [all these things].
But seek first the kingdom of God and His righteousness,
and all these things will be provided for you.

MATTHEW 6:32–33

_____
_____
_____
_____
_____
_____
_____
_____
_____
_____
_____
_____
_____
_____

O Lord, help me to channel today's energy into worshiping You and doing the work You've given me to do right now. I love You and have faith that You will keep Your promise to provide in my future—because You know what I need long before I do.

WHAT MOTIVATES YOU?

Fear is a motivator when knowledge and understanding are lacking. For example, say a brand-new opportunity arises that could be *amazing*, but the more you think about it, the more you realize there are too many questions and unknowns. You think, *I haven't done that before; I've never been there before.* So, you decline. Your decision is motivated by fear of the unknown rather than confidence based on what is known.

Knowledge is power—power to cast out fear from any situation. It is understanding that enables us to make sound decisions for a lifetime. Lack of knowledge about a person or situation allows the enemy to instill fear and doubt. It's why he wants to keep us ignorant of God, which happens when we don't prioritize time with Him to know Him through prayer and the promises in His Word.

Let us make time to know Him well—and live boldly in His power!

---

*The Lord gives wisdom; from his mouth come knowledge
and understanding; he stores up sound wisdom for the upright;
he is a shield to those who walk in integrity.*

PROVERBS 2:6–7 ESV

*Accept My instruction instead of silver,
and knowledge rather than pure gold.*

PROVERBS 8:10

*The Lord looks down from heaven upon the children of men,
to see if there are any who understand, who seek God.*

PSALM 14:2 NKJV

*His divine power has given us everything required
for life and godliness through the knowledge of Him
who called us by His own glory and goodness.*

II PETER 1:3

---

*Lord, I want to make sound decisions from the power that You give. The next time
I'm about to turn away from opportunities in fear, please stop me. Help me to see
Your truth and make decisions based on the clarity it brings.*

CONFESSION SETS YOU FREE

Most spiders are nocturnal creatures, which means they come out in the dark of night to hunt while their predators are asleep. And if you're like most people, just the thought of stepping on a spider when getting out of bed at night evokes a flash of fear (maybe even a scream!). Well, fear and sin are a lot like spiders. Holding onto a sin—even a little one—means inhabiting darkness, and darkness is where fear roams. While you may be dull, or even asleep, to a certain sin in your life, fear is thriving on it. Fear in disobedience, fear of getting caught, fear of consequences... This is why confession of sin is so vital to combating fear. Repentance shines light and dispels all darkness, and fear no longer has a home. Let us search our hearts and confess any sin we find there.

There will be more joy in heaven over one sinner who repents
than over ninety-nine righteous people who don't need repentance.

LUKE 15:7

I will brighten the darkness before them and smooth out the road
ahead of them. Yes, I will indeed do these things; I will not forsake them.

ISAIAH 42:16 NLT

The one who walks in darkness doesn't know where he's going.

JOHN 12:35

I confess my iniquity; I am anxious because of my sin.

PSALM 38:18

_____
_____
_____
_____
_____
_____
_____
_____
_____
_____
_____
_____
_____
_____
_____
_____
_____
_____

Lord, today I come clean. I no longer want to feed fear. I confess to You now
_____ *. I ask Your forgiveness*
and ask that You create in me a clean heart. I want to live in Your light,
where sin and fear cannot have a hold on me.

REJECT YOUR REJECTION

The pain of rejection is a pain like no other. It's a pain that can go far beneath the surface and into the very depths of one's soul. When we love someone who doesn't love us back; when we've applied for jobs and don't get them; when we invite friends to a celebration and no one shows… We all have a badge of scars with *REJECTION* stamped on top, and that badge feeds our fear of adding yet another mark. What's wonderful is, we don't have to wear the badge. We can say "no" to the power of rejection's grip and receive the holy love and acceptance that Jesus gives. He knew the ultimate rejection, yet every day He continues to call us to Himself. We have the authority to put His voice of love over the lures of fear and soak in the healing balm of His grace. Will you answer His call?

So honor will come to you who believe; but for the unbelieving, the stone that the builders rejected—this one has become the cornerstone, and a stone to stumble over, and a rock to trip over.

I PETER 2:7–8

Some have rejected these [instructions] and have shipwrecked their faith.

I TIMOTHY 1:19

Then [Jesus] began to tell [the disciples] about the terrible things He would suffer, and that He would be rejected by the elders and the chief priests and the other Jewish leaders.

MARK 8:31 TLB

_____

_____

_____

_____

_____

_____

_____

_____

_____

_____

_____

_____

_____

Lord, rejection hurts. My heart seems constantly in need of Your healing grace over its pain and scars. Yet when I think of the rejection You faced on the cross— and still face today—I know You understand and have compassion. I receive You and claim the healing You provide. I believe and live for Your love, today and for always.

SHARING THE GOSPEL

Getting rejected, even persecuted, for sharing the gospel is nothing new under the sun. Jesus Himself was rejected, so we would be remiss to think we won't be. Approaching an unbeliever about faith can be both frightening and unnerving—we never know what their response might be. Yet it is our very faith that keeps us strong and steadfast to keep doing it. That's because Jesus didn't provide the gospel for us to memorize for ourselves; He gave us power, and the command, to speak it—the very power He knew we'd need to be bold, steady, and assured. Claim that power for yourself today, and every day. Be ready to spread the truth and hold on to the joy that is yours when you do.

---

*Our gospel did not come to you in word only,
but also in power, in the Holy Spirit, and with full assurance.*

I THESSALONIANS 1:5

*Therefore, let us approach the throne of grace with boldness,
so that we may receive mercy and find grace to help us in time of need.*

HEBREWS 4:16

*In spite of severe persecution, you welcomed the message with joy
from the Holy Spirit. As a result, you became an example
to all the believers.... For the word of the Lord rang out from you...
in every place that your faith in God has gone out.*

I THESSALONIANS 1:6–8

You are the light of the world. A city situated on a hill cannot be hidden. No one lights a lamp and puts it under a basket, but rather on a lampstand, and it gives light for all who are in the house.

MATTHEW 5:14–15

_____

_____

_____

_____

_____

_____

_____

_____

_____

_____

_____

_____

_____

_____

Lord, sharing Your gospel message is hard because so many people don't want to hear it. But there are many who do, and I want to be ready to share with them, no matter the cost. I draw on Your power today to speak in love and without apology. You saved my life, and I want others to be saved too.

SHAKE OFF THE DUST

When we share our faith with unbelievers, we set ourselves up for rejection. Sometimes we don't even have to share—we can simply be seen with a Bible in hand or a framed verse sitting on our desk. The anticipated rejection, scoffing, ending of friendships, and slamming of doors not only hurt our feelings but also our confidence to be used by God. Fear of sharing our testimony can rise up in no time and lead to feeling inadequate in our faith. But when Jesus sent His disciples out to share the Good News, He not only knew they'd be rejected, He didn't coddle their feelings about it. He simply said to shake off the dust from their feet and move on. This doesn't mean we aren't to love our neighbors—that is the second greatest commandment. But we are to move on for the sake of those who *do* want to hear about Jesus' love. May we not miss them!

Paul and Barnabas shook the dust off their feet against them and went to Iconium. And the disciples were filled with joy and the Holy Spirit.

ACTS 13:51–52

Whoever listens to you listens to Me. Whoever rejects you rejects Me. And whoever rejects Me rejects the one who sent me.

LUKE 10:16

If someone won't welcome you or listen to your message, leave their home or town. And shake the dust from your feet at them.

MATTHEW 10:14 CEV

*If they do not welcome you, when you leave that town,
shake off the dust from your feet as a testimony against them.*

LUKE 9:5

_____

_____

_____

_____

_____

_____

_____

_____

_____

_____

_____

_____

_____

_____

_____

_____

_____

*Lord, thank You for this. Thank You for freeing me of the weight and burden
I've felt when people have rejected me because I love You. Thank You for releasing
me of others' responses to the gospel. Help me to remember that it's You they're
rejecting, which is the ultimate tragedy that saddens my heart.*

FEAR OF HEIGHTS

For some, the thought of looking down from the top of a ladder, a building, or a cliff turns their stomach and makes them hold a death grip on anything within reach. But physical heights are only one height to fear: there are spiritual heights that beckon as well. When we look up and hear God calling—to new plateaus of service, a different ministry, maybe even a move to a different country—that's when the words *impossible!* and *I'm not qualified!* play over and over in our minds. But scaling up to new heights is what this Christian life is about—being used in ways we can't even imagine. Fear and doubt are Satan's way of holding us back. Thankfully, we are not left to scale alone. God promises to equip and empower, lead and guide the willing, obedient, and trusting heart. Be ready to climb, and do not fear in the process!

He makes me sure-footed as a deer; He keeps me safe on the mountains.

PSALM 18:33 GNT

*But You, LORD, are a shield around me, my glory,
and the one who lifts up my head. I cry aloud to the LORD,
and He answers me from His holy mountain.*

PSALM 3:3-4

*Everyone who lives on milk is inexperienced with the message
about righteousness, because he is an infant. But solid food
is for the mature—for those whose senses have been trained
to distinguish between good and evil.*

HEBREWS 5:13-14

Therefore let us get past the elementary stage in the teachings about the Christ, advancing on to maturity and perfection and spiritual completeness.

HEBREWS 6:1 AMP

Lord, I confess that sometimes I just want to stay comfortable in my spiritual walk. It's scary to face the changes needed for true growth in You. Please give me the courage and the desire to climb toward a higher level of service for You.

HE HELPS IN OUR WEAKNESS

One fear common to humankind since the beginning of time is that of public speaking. Standing center stage, making a presentation, sharing the gospel with a crowd—the thought alone can ignite a panic attack in an instant. Moses *really* struggled with this. He was far from eloquent and very uncomfortable in the spotlight, yet God continually put him in a position to speak. Being used by God in any area of weakness is terrifying. But this is the beautiful unpredictability of our God and yet one more way He displays His power, His plan, and His grace. He holds the gifts we need—and imparts them to us as we need them. If He has you there right now, believe and trust that God is with you, and He *will* help, just like He helped Moses.

———

The Lord said to [Moses], "Who placed a mouth on humans? Who makes a person mute or deaf, seeing or blind? Is it not I, the Lord? Now go! I will help you speak and I will teach you what to say." Moses said, "Please, Lord, send someone else."

EXODUS 4:11–13

Though he falls, he will not be overwhelmed, because the Lord supports him with His hand.

PSALM 37:24

You [the disciples] will even be brought before governors and kings... to bear witness to them and to the Gentiles. But...don't worry about how or what you are to speak. For you will be given what to say at that hour, because it isn't you speaking, but the Spirit of your Father is speaking through you.

MATTHEW 10:18–20

But Moses said to the LORD, "Oh, my Lord, I am not eloquent, either in the past or since you have spoken to your servant, but I am slow of speech and of tongue."

EXODUS 4:10 ESV

_____
_____
_____
_____
_____
_____
_____
_____
_____
_____
_____
_____
_____
_____
_____
_____
_____

O Lord, thank You that You don't call us to do something, then leave us to accomplish it on our own. Your grace was sufficient for Moses, and it is sufficient for me. And I am so grateful.

KEEP REACHING

This story...it is full of faith beyond measure. A woman had suffered miserably for twelve long years. She had tried everything possible for a cure, but nothing helped. But then she entered the presence of Jesus. She had to fight through a crowd, but she didn't give up. She didn't try to get His attention. She didn't ask to approach Him. She didn't make eye contact. She didn't even speak to Him. She simply believed in His power to heal and braced herself to receive it. Then she reached for His tassel. She reached...

Are you fighting through a crowd of doubt today? Are you reaching for the Savior of your soul? Reach, and keep reaching and believing that God is with you and that He cares. Touch the tassel of His presence and He *will* help you.

For I, Yahweh your God, hold your right hand and say to you:
Do not fear, I will help you.

ISAIAH 41:13 HCSB

Then Jesus told the centurion,
"Go. As you have believed, let it be done for you."
And his servant was healed that very moment.

MATTHEW 8:13

After looking directly at [the lame man] and seeing that he had faith
to be healed, Paul said in a loud voice, "Stand up on your feet!"
And he jumped up and began to walk around.

ACTS 14:9–10

*A woman suffering from bleeding...approached from behind
and touched the tassel of His robe. Instantly her bleeding stopped.
"Who touched Me?" Jesus asked.... "Daughter," He said to her,
"your faith has made you well."*

LUKE 8:43–45, 48 HCSB

_____

_____

_____

_____

_____

_____

_____

_____

_____

_____

_____

_____

_____

_____

_____

_____

*O Lord, I reach for You today. My hands and heart are outstretched with longing
for Your warm embrace and healing power. Please take what faith I have
and multiply Your goodness for a brand-new hope that cannot be quenched,
no matter what I face.*

FEAR PAST AND PRESENT

Fear is our past being invited into the present. I'm talking about the agonizing failures and painful regrets from months, years, even lifetimes ago. They play into the present and dance a slow death around our hopes for a brighter future. It's where fear reigned then and wants to reign now. Remembering isn't wrong or bad, but what we recall and dwell on determines the presence of fear or the presence of power—God's power—for today. So remember what God has done and believe that His love for you hasn't waned—it only burns *stronger*. You are His beloved, and He will bless you and keep you in His righteous right hand forever.

———

I will remember the LORD's works;
yes, I will remember Your ancient wonders.
I will reflect on all You have done
and meditate on Your actions.

PSALM 77:11–12

Seek the LORD and His strength; seek His face always.
Remember the wondrous works He has done, His wonders,
and the judgments He has pronounced.

PSALM 105:4–5

LORD our God, lords other than You have owned us,
but we remember Your name alone.

ISAIAH 26:13

Jesus said, "You of little faith, why are you discussing
among yourselves that you do not have bread?...
Don't you remember the five loaves for the five thousand
and how many baskets you collected?"

MATTHEW 16:8–9

Lord, You have been so faithful to me in the past. Help my focus to stay on all that You have done, all the ways You've blessed me. Since You have shown Your love before, I know You are with me now and in the days and years ahead.

THE POWER OF FEAR, THE POWER OF JESUS

Fear has the power to make us do all sorts of things we wouldn't normally do and to act out in ways that surprise even ourselves. Such as lash out in anger when we are usually calm. Or lie about something when we have a history of integrity. Or run from problems when we're known to persevere through them.

Jesus also has the power to make us do all sorts of things we wouldn't normally do. Such as hold our tongue when someone's attacking us. Possess peace and calm in seemingly hopeless situations. And respond to someone who's acting out in fear with love, mercy, and forgiveness.

Let's make a difference and choose the power of Jesus today to help those who are living in fear to know Him in a whole new way. Let's cover the power of fear with the power of Jesus.

"Which of these three do you think proved to be a neighbor to the man who fell into the hands of the robbers?" [Jesus asked.] "The one who showed mercy to him," he said. Then Jesus told him, "Go and do the same."

LUKE 10:36–37

Mercy triumphs over judgment.

JAMES 2:13

God had mercy on me so that Christ Jesus could use me as an example to show everyone how patient He is with even the worst sinners, so that others will realize that they, too, can have everlasting life.

I TIMOTHY 1:16 TLB

Now you have every grace and blessing; every spiritual gift and power for doing His will are yours during this time of waiting for the return of our Lord Jesus Christ.

I CORINTHIANS 1:7 TLB

_____
_____
_____
_____
_____
_____
_____
_____
_____
_____
_____
_____
_____
_____
_____

O Lord, stop me the next time I start to judge someone because their actions are brow-raising. Give me the eyes to see what they're really struggling with and the heart to respond with mercy and understanding. Goodness knows You've given me the same response at times; now help me to do the same for others.

WHEN ALL SEEMS LOST

Have you ever worked toward something, whether for days, months, or years, excited to see the final result, only to experience disaster? Time, money, energy, talent—all lost, and for what? It's only natural to feel downcast and fear that your loss can never be recovered. But this is a lie Satan would have you believe. Yes, there may be loss, but don't think the immediate result is the end result. Our God is a redeeming God. He is a Master at creating beauty from ashes, the oil of gladness instead of mourning, a garment of praise instead of despair. Nothing, absolutely *nothing* in God's economy is wasted. His presence in any circumstance truly does work all things for the good of those who love Him. It's a promise.

He has sent me to bind up the brokenhearted,
to proclaim liberty to the captives...
to give them a beautiful headdress instead of ashes,
the oil of gladness instead of mourning,
the garment of praise instead of a faint spirit.

ISAIAH 61:1, 3 ESV

I will repay you for the years that the swarming locust ate.

JOEL 2:25

The God of all grace, who called you to His eternal glory in Christ,
will Himself restore, establish, strengthen, and support you
after you have suffered a little while.

I PETER 5:10

We know that God is always at work
for the good of everyone who loves Him.

ROMANS 8:28 CEV

Father, it's hard not to be discouraged when standing in defeat—in a place and time when so much appears to be lost. But I will trust in You...to redeem the time, the energy, the resources—both physical and emotional—that appear to be wasted. I know You have a plan for my good, so I will trust in You.

KING OF GLORY

Soon after Pharaoh released the Israelites from years of slavery, he wouldn't let them go far without a fight. And God knew it. He also knew that, because of the Israelites' weak emotional condition, they'd run back to Egypt in order to avoid war. So God led them in an unexpected direction—through the wilderness. On the outside it looked as though they were headed for death, yet God was setting up circumstances for a miracle we still talk about today: the parting of the Red Sea. Just when defeat looked imminent, God delivered His people and stole the show in the process—because not everything was about them. And not everything is about us today. If only we could remember this! God will use our difficulties to show that His majesty still reigns, and that He wants the glory. We have only to trust, obey, and watch for His hand of deliverance.

So He led the people around toward the Red Sea along the road of the wilderness.... The Israelites were terrified and cried out to the LORD for help.

EXODUS 13:18; 14:10

So the crowd was amazed when they saw those unable to speak talking, the crippled restored, the lame walking, and the blind seeing, and they gave glory to the God of Israel.

MATTHEW 15:31

Who is this King of glory? The LORD, strong and mighty, the LORD, mighty in battle.

PSALM 24:8

*The Egyptians will know that I am Yahweh
when I receive glory through Pharaoh.*

EXODUS 14:18 HCSB

_____

_____

_____

_____

_____

_____

_____

_____

_____

_____

_____

_____

_____

_____

_____

_____

*Father, forgive me for trying to figure out my own solutions to my problems
and fears. No matter how bleak things seem now, I want to walk in faith and trust
that You have an amazing plan that is for my good and for Your glory, not mine.
May all praise be to You.*

WRITE ON GOD'S HEART

One benefit of technology today is that employers can automatically deposit our paychecks directly into our bank accounts. Once we sign our approval and the data is set up in their system, they automatically deposit the amount we've agreed to work for. Then we can pay bills and go shopping knowing that the money is there. This is much the same when you choose to believe God for more faith in the power of Jesus—the exact amount needed for the circumstance you are in. Your faith ignites your signature on His heart and keeps the blessing of faith flowing for as long and as much as you need. Will you write on His heart today and trust? He is faithful to do what He promises to do.

For this is the covenant that I will make
with the house of Israel after those days, says the Lord:
I will put my laws into their minds
and write them on their hearts.
I will be their God, and they will be my people.

HEBREWS 8:10

Guard the deposit entrusted to you.

I TIMOTHY 6:20 ESV

A manifestation of the Spirit is given to each person
for the common good: to one is given a message of wisdom...
to another, faith by the same Spirit....One and the same Spirit
is active in all these, distributing to each person as He wills.

I CORINTHIANS 12:7-9, 11

_____
_____
_____
_____
_____
_____
_____
_____
_____
_____
_____
_____
_____
_____
_____
_____

Father, I want to write on Your heart. I choose to believe the promises in Your Word. I will walk by faith today knowing You are with me. I trust that You'll provide more than I need for working through the challenges You know will come.

THE ROOT OF FEAR

Fear on any level finds its roots in the spiritual realm. There are evil rulers, demonic authorities, and dark world powers in an equation that adds up to one thing: war for our souls. There are multitudes of armies, battalions, and troops on the attack with no job other than to instill fear, discouragement, defeat, depression, and hopelessness into our hearts and minds.

Praise God that He reigns! Praise God He is stronger and has the *ultimate authority* over all. And praise God for His armor—to shield and deflect the efforts of the enemy from every angle. Praise God that He receives our prayers and delivers us upon request. Let us all remember to praise and clothe ourselves *every day* with the power, strength, endurance, and faith that is ours as God leads us to victory one day at a time.

Simon, Simon, look out! Satan has asked to sift you like wheat. But I have prayed for you that your faith may not fail.

LUKE 22:31–32

Be serious! Be alert! Your adversary the Devil is prowling around like a roaring lion, looking for anyone he can devour. Resist him and be firm in the faith.

I PETER 5:8–9 HCSB

God's Word is an indispensable weapon. In the same way, prayer is essential in this ongoing warfare. Pray hard and long. Pray for your brothers and sisters. Keep your eyes open.

EPHESIANS 6:17 THE MESSAGE

For our battle is not against flesh and blood,
but against the rulers, against the authorities,
against the world powers of this darkness,
against the spiritual forces of evil in the heavens.

EPHESIANS 6:12 HCSB

_____

_____

_____

_____

_____

_____

_____

_____

_____

_____

_____

_____

_____

_____

Father, thank You for Your armor! Thank You for the power I have through prayer.
I ask You to clothe me in it today, especially with Your shield of faith. Guard my
head, my heart, my body, and my spirit, keeping Your grace, love, and peace
in and the enemy's evil attacks out.

A SUPERNATURAL APPEAL

Weakness and fear go hand in hand. We grow tired and weak when we are afraid, and we become afraid when we are tired and weak. Tied together, they quickly spiral us down into discouragement and hopelessness. What is a person to do? Move from a natural stance of strength to a supernatural position of appeal. When we are weak on our knees in the posture of prayer, God moves in and activates His power in us to do more than we ever imagined. Belief in *His* strength creates the platform for His power in you and in me that is so breathtaking, there's no mistaking Whose power it is. Then hope is restored and strength is renewed. His ability is His promise to us, and He keeps His promises. We just have to ask and then believe.

[Abraham] did not waver in unbelief at God's promise
but was strengthened in his faith and gave glory to God,
because he was fully convinced that what God had promised,
He was also able to do.

ROMANS 4:20–21

He gives strength to the faint and strengthens the powerless.

ISAIAH 40:29

The LORD is my strength and my shield; my heart trusts in Him,
and I am helped.... The LORD is the strength of His people;
He is a stronghold of salvation for His anointed.

PSALM 28:7–8

I pray that He may grant you, according to the riches of His glory,
to be strengthened with power in your inner being through His Spirit,
and that Christ may dwell in your hearts through faith.

EPHESIANS 3:16–17

Father, life gets so busy and full, I long for real rest and renewal for my soul.
Please part the pages of my calendar and help me to be still and refresh my heart.
Fill me with Your strength, and help me complete the work You've given me to do.

FEAR GOD

When we think about fear in general, there's usually a negative connotation. But not all fear is bad—there is fear we should actually embrace with passion and ferocity. It is the fear of God. Not the kind that makes us cower and want to run, but a reverent fear that calls us to bow and acknowledge His greatness. It's a humble and grateful heart that feeds from the utmost respect and awe of the Creator of the universe. He provides for our needs, pours out His mercy, forgives our sins, covers us with grace, and loves us with an unshakable bond. Speak with praise and worship His holiness…and consider the fear of God.

Happy is the person who fears the Lord,
taking great delight in His commands.
His descendants will be powerful in the land;
the generation of the upright will be blessed.

PSALM 112:1–2

The reverence and fear of God are basic to all wisdom.

PROVERBS 9:10 TLB

The Lord keeps His eye on those who fear Him—
those who depend on His faithful love.

PSALM 33:18

Above all, fear the LORD and worship Him faithfully
with all your heart; consider the great things He has done for you.

I SAMUEL 12:24

_____

_____

_____

_____

_____

_____

_____

_____

_____

_____

_____

_____

_____

_____

_____

_____

*Father, I love You, worship You, and revere Your holy name. I'm glad I have
nothing to fear in Your presence and everything to gain. I look up to You
in the heavens and know that You are my God—my faithful and loving Lord.
Nothing compares with You.*

NEVER GIVE UP!

We are in a battle every day. We can't see it, but there's a spiritual battle that rages in every believer's life. People often think that becoming a Christian means an easier life, but in fact, it gets harder in many ways. With every conversion, every prayer, every testimony that plants seeds of faith in others, Satan will try to hinder those seeds from falling on soft hearts and sprouting new love for the Savior. He will try to stop grounded believers from growing in their faith at every turn. When we are doing *anything* to enhance and further God's kingdom, the enemy is there to put up a fight. We can *expect* resistance rather than be confused by it. Praise God that He doesn't leave us to battle alone. He is with us, and we have His very armor to protect us. It's what empowers us never to give up, which is what the enemy wants. Never give up!

We wanted to come to you—even I, Paul, time and again—
but Satan hindered us.

I THESSALONIANS 2:18

"Don't be afraid, Daniel," [an angel] said to me, "for from the first day
that you purposed to understand and to humble yourself before your God,
your prayers were heard. I have come because of your prayers.
But the prince of the kingdom of Persia opposed me for twenty-one days."

DANIEL 10:12–13

We must be serious and put on the armor of faith
and love on our chests, and put on a helmet of the hope of salvation.

I THESSALONIANS 5:8 HCSB

Be strengthened by the Lord and by His vast strength.
Put on the full armor of God so that you can stand against
the tactics of the Devil. For our battle is not against
flesh and blood, but against the rulers, against the authorities,
against the world powers of this darkness,
against the spiritual forces of evil in the heavens.

EPHESIANS 6:10–12 HCSB

_____

_____

_____

_____

_____

_____

_____

_____

_____

_____

_____

_____

_____

_____

Father, I am so glad and comforted to know I am not alone in my daily battles—
You are with me, and I have Your power to face them. I clothe myself now
with Your full armor, to strengthen and help me stand firm and not give up.

WAIT IN PRAYER

Fear is a constant companion in our waiting rooms. It whispers, "God hasn't answered your prayer because He doesn't care." Or, "God is not in control, *you* are." And, "Stop waiting for Him and do what you think is best because He's busy helping someone else." These lies can make waiting feel like a slow, dull knife cut. But when our waiting rooms turn into prayer rooms, fear cannot survive—its voice goes mute. Prayers release an incense of trust, belief, faith, and love that fear cannot be part of. So turn your waiting into the pleasing aroma of prayer. God hears and cares about every word, every petition. He is with you, and He *will* answer in His perfect timing and way.

The Lord is far from the wicked,
but He hears the prayer of the righteous.

PROVERBS 15:29

I waited patiently for the Lord,
and He turned to me and heard my cry for help.
He brought me up from a desolate pit,
out of the muddy clay, and set my feet on a rock,
making my steps secure.

PSALM 40:1–2

When you pray, go into your private room, shut your door, and pray to your Father who is in secret. And your Father who sees in secret will reward you.

MATTHEW 6:6

_____
_____
_____
_____
_____
_____
_____
_____
_____
_____
_____
_____
_____
_____
_____
_____

Lord, I pray for Your peace and patience while I wait. Help me be content and focused on the work of my hands until Your answers come. Help me to truly embrace and live in Your faithful love that doesn't grow dim.

GOD'S WORD IS ALIVE

God's Word—it's powerful and active and a very present help in times of trouble. It's where God speaks directly to us and provides answers to the problems we're facing. So, if we have access to what we need for navigating through today's battles, why don't more of us read it every day? If it were announced that the IRS had just mailed out $10,000 refund checks, we'd *all* make sure to look in our mailboxes until that check was in our hands! An even greater gift awaits us within the pages of the Bible, yet we don't have enough time...we're too busy... The enemy not only creates the fears we harbor, he also keeps us distracted from the solutions for eliminating them. God's Word is effective to dispel *all* of our fears. But even more, God longs to share Himself and the love He has with each and every heart that will listen.

For the word of God is living and effective and sharper than any double-edged sword, penetrating as far as the separation of soul and spirit, joints and marrow.

HEBREWS 4:12

Take the helmet of salvation and the sword of the Spirit— which is the word of God.

EPHESIANS 6:17

With you I can attack a barricade, and with my God I can leap over a wall. God—His way is perfect; the word of the LORD is pure. He is a shield to all who take refuge in Him.

PSALM 18:29–30

You veterans know the One who started it all;
and you newcomers—such vitality and strength!
God's word is so steady in you. Your fellowship with God
enables you to gain a victory over the Evil One.

I JOHN 2:14 THE MESSAGE

_____
_____
_____
_____
_____
_____
_____
_____
_____
_____
_____
_____
_____
_____

Father, thank You for Your Word—as a guide, a light, and a source for knowing You and accessing the power I have through You. Forgive me for not reading it as often and fervently as I should. Help me to discipline my time so that we get time alone together every day.

FEAR FOR OUR GOOD

Some fear is for our own good. It comes from the conviction we feel when we're disobedient to God. While Paul was in prison, Felix sent for him to talk about life in Christ. As Paul spoke of Jesus and the judgment to come, Felix became afraid—not because of what Paul was saying, but because of what Felix wasn't doing. He was already versed enough to know that Paul spoke truth, but Felix's head knowledge didn't convert into his heart and lifestyle. When God tells us to live one way and we choose another, conviction evolves into fear—fear of separation from God and fear of the consequences for our disobedience. Fear of ignoring a conviction is an important guide for us to heed to help us stay on God's perfect path to peace. It's fear that is for our good. Do you have a conviction?

Whoever doubts stands condemned if he eats,
because his eating is not from a conviction,
and everything that is not from a conviction is sin.

ROMANS 14:23 HCSB

Encourage one another daily, as long as it is called "Today,"
so that none of you may be hardened by sin's deceitfulness.
We have come to share in Christ, if indeed we hold
our original conviction firmly to the very end.

HEBREWS 3:13–14 NIV

I have swept away your transgressions like a cloud,
and your sins like a mist. Return to Me, for I have redeemed you.

ISAIAH 44:22

[Felix] sent for Paul and listened to him on the subject of faith in Christ Jesus. Now as he spoke about righteousness, self-control, and the judgment to come, Felix became afraid....

ACTS 24:24–25

_____
_____
_____
_____
_____
_____
_____
_____
_____
_____
_____
_____
_____
_____
_____

Lord, I am so grateful You don't leave me to myself. I'm grateful for the convictions You impart whenever I stray and for knowing that You wait with loving arms each time for my return.

SING YOUR OWN SONG

Have you ever heard a mockingbird sing? It is amazing at imitating other bird songs. It can recreate dozens of melodies and sounds and string them together into one long, beautiful piece of music. The thing is, it doesn't sing its own songs. This is much like what we do when we act or speak or perform for others in order to be accepted on their terms. Doing this stems from fear of rejection—or wanting to be accepted at the sacrifice of ourselves. But God gave each of us our own song to sing. And we will never know just how beautiful and unique we are if we compromise our song for the sake of someone else's unmerited and temporal favor. God made each of us to sing our God-given song to Him and to others for His glory. So, have courage—sing your *own* song.

*Body and soul, I am marvelously made! I worship in adoration—
what a creation! You know me inside and out, You know every bone
in my body; You know exactly how I was made, bit by bit,
how I was sculpted from nothing into something.*

PSALM 139:13 THE MESSAGE

*Listen to me, you who know righteousness,
the people in whose heart is My instruction:
do not fear disgrace by men,
and do not be shattered by their taunts.*

ISAIAH 51:7

I, even I, am He who comforts you and gives you all this joy.
So what right have you to fear mere mortal men,
who wither like the grass and disappear?

ISAIAH 51:12 TLB

_____
_____
_____
_____
_____
_____
_____
_____
_____
_____
_____
_____
_____
_____

Lord, forgive me for all the times I've gone along with the crowd or not spoken my true and honest thoughts out of fear of rejection. Help me to think and to act, to worship and live as You lead, not as others lead. Help me to be who You made me to be—to embrace my person and calling the way You created me. Help me to truly believe that I am beautiful, just as I am.

DO IT AFRAID

Are you waiting for fear to subside before taking the next steps toward a dream? Are you hoping your fear will dissipate before moving toward fulfilling God's call on your life? Waiting and hoping are not bad. It's good to be cautious and wise—as long as you're sure that's what God is telling you to do. But if He is the one waiting on you, it's different. Your disobedience can actually be adding to your fear. So if the latter is the case, do it afraid. Take the first step in spite of your fear. As soon as you do, trust Him to fill you with courage, even excitement, and help you in ways you never thought possible. He will be faithful to help and to hold you together, because He will not abandon those in whom He lives—and He lives in you.

Even when we are too weak to have any faith left,
He remains faithful to us and will help us,
for He cannot disown us who are part of Himself,
and He will always carry out His promises to us.

II TIMOTHY 2:13 TLB

He said to me, "My grace is sufficient for you, for my power is perfected
in weakness." Therefore, I [Paul] will most gladly boast all the more
about my weaknesses, so that Christ's power may reside in me.

II CORINTHIANS 12:9

[Jesus] was crucified in weakness, but He lives by the power of God.
For we also are weak in Him, but in dealing with you
we will live with Him by God's power.

II CORINTHIANS 13:4

I am the LORD your God, who holds your right hand...
I will help you.

ISAIAH 41:13

Lord, forgive me for any of the ways I've held back from Your leading because
I listened to my fear more than I relied on You. Be with me now as I take steps
toward the convictions I know You've placed in my heart. I hold fast to Your
promise to help me.

HAVE FAITH IN GOD

It's been said that if your faith is dependent on a certain outcome, you are sure to lose it. So if God answers a prayer and your faith is conditioned to the answer, be assured your faith will shrink. If faith is placed on a condition rather than in God, it will fail because He is the only immovable, infallible source of fullness there is.

God's ways don't always make sense, but they are always good. His answers aren't always what we want to hear, but they are what they are for our best welfare. His provision, no matter what form it takes, is perfect—always. Whatever He does is life-building and meant to increase our love and trust in Him who is faithful to the very end—even when we aren't. So put faith where it belongs: not in a man-made condition but in our all-powerful God of creation.

Love the LORD your God, obey Him, and remain faithful to Him.
For He is your life, and He will prolong your days
as you live in the land the LORD swore to give
to your fathers Abraham, Isaac, and Jacob.

DEUTERONOMY 30:20

If some were unfaithful, will their unfaithfulness
nullify God's faithfulness? Absolutely not!

ROMANS 3:3–4

Your faithful love is higher than the heavens, and Your faithfulness
reaches to the clouds. God, be exalted above the heavens,
and let Your glory be over the whole earth.

PSALM 108:4–5

Jesus replied to them, "Have faith in God."

MARK 11:22

_____

_____

_____

_____

_____

_____

_____

_____

_____

_____

_____

_____

_____

_____

_____

_____

_____

_____

_____

Father, looking back, I can see times I've put my faith in other people and things that were not of You, and I harbor disappointment to this day. Please forgive me. Help me realign my faith in You and only You.

CHANGE IS...

Every single day can bring change we never saw coming. Some changes are slow and drawn out; others are swift and jolting. But however they occur, they're often a testing of our faith, because God's current provision doesn't yet match our set of upcoming needs. Our capacity for figuring out the details doesn't match up to the list of new unknowns. They are also times when the beauty of God's power and provision gets unveiled— through an outpouring of prayer and acknowledgment that we are not as in control as we thought. Could it be this is why God allows changes to keep coming? So we'll remember and know that He is God, and that He doesn't change? His faithfulness is a wind that keeps blowing into every sail of need we open up to Him. How comforting to know that He is our very present help through every change life brings.

Every good and perfect gift is from above,
coming down from the Father of lights,
who does not change like shifting shadows.

JAMES 1:17

I provide water in the wilderness, and rivers in the desert,
to give drink to My chosen people.
The people I formed for Myself will declare My praise.

ISAIAH 43:20–21

Your Father knows the things you need before you ask Him.

MATTHEW 6:8

_____
_____
_____
_____
_____
_____
_____
_____
_____
_____
_____
_____
_____
_____
_____
_____
_____
_____

Lord, You are my calm amidst the constant changes of life. I don't know what tomorrow holds, but You do, and You know what I'll need to get through. Thank You for being my ever-present help and stronghold. I rest in You, knowing You are for me and that You will provide.

PRAISE THE NAME OF JESUS

If there's one thing Satan hates to hear more than the name of Jesus, it's hearing it said in praise—through worship, song, and prayers of thanksgiving. That's because, when we praise God, our attention goes to His presence, His goodness, and most of all, His love. And "perfect love drives out fear" (I John 4:18). Through His perfection, no weapon formed against us can prosper, and that includes the ugly forces of fear. Even the demons know and understand the power of His light and love, so much so they cringe and flee at the mere mention of His name.

Whatever demons are harassing you today, ward them off with the power of a name: *Jesus*! Shout goodbye to them with boldness as you welcome the Savior into your heart and release your tongue with praise.

Even the demons believe—and they shudder.

JAMES 2:19

On the basis of faith in His name, it is the name of Jesus which has strengthened this man whom you see and know; and the faith which comes through Him has given him this perfect health and complete wholeness in your presence.

ACTS 3:16 AMP

Let them praise the name of the LORD, for His name alone is exalted. His majesty covers heaven and earth.

PSALM 148:13

There is no fear in love; instead, perfect love drives out fear, because fear involves punishment. So the one who fears is not complete in love.

I JOHN 4:18

_____
_____
_____
_____
_____
_____
_____
_____
_____
_____
_____
_____
_____
_____

Jesus! I call to You today and claim Your power and presence in my life. I lift my praise and command the enemies of fear, discouragement, doubt, and everything else that holds me down to flee. I breathe in more of You and rejoice with a song in my heart for the peace and rest that only You can give.

BELIEVE GOD

We all go through seasons of challenge that pull, twist, and squeeze our faith jar one drop at a time. It's those times we think, *God, I need more faith. Please give me more faith!* This leads one to ask, Just how *do* you get more faith? That is, at least enough to be at rest and filled with peace, in spite of your circumstances. The answer is simple: believe God. Call to Him with the knowledge that He is the supplier of all that you need, and then *believe* that He will indeed provide. Abraham believed God, and faith was credited—or deposited—to him for righteousness (James 2:23).

When you believe, the floodgates are opened, and more faith is credited to you as well. You must simply take Him at His Word and believe.

Let us hold on to the confession of our hope without wavering,
since He who promised is faithful.

HEBREWS 10:23

Yes, my soul, find rest in God; my hope comes from Him.
Truly He is my rock and my salvation;
He is my fortress, I will not be shaken.

PSALM 62:5–6 NIV

"How were your eyes opened?" [The blind man] answered, "The man
called Jesus made mud, spread it on my eyes, and told me,
'Go to Siloam and wash.' So when I went and washed I received my sight."

JOHN 9:10–11

Abraham believed God, and it was credited to him
for righteousness, and he was called God's friend.

JAMES 2:23

_____

_____

_____

_____

_____

_____

_____

_____

_____

_____

_____

_____

_____

_____

_____

_____

Father, I call to You now for Your Spirit to pour into mine an abundance of faith for what I am facing. You have been faithful to me in the past, and I know You will be faithful to me now to see me through. I believe!

THAT FOUR-LETTER WORD

Our culture is unapologetically loud about having things our way, doing what we want, having our own mind, and questioning authority. The word *obey* has become synonymous with slavery and abuse, yet God uses that four-letter word in His Word. He clearly says we are to obey His commands. Jesus calls us to obey His teachings. To obey means to submit, to allow something or someone to lead and direct our day-to-day living.

We are all submitting to something, and it's usually to what we love—either the world and its ways or righteousness in God. As believers, our heartfelt love for our gracious Lord is the driving force that grows our desire to let Him lead. When we live by His teachings, we are filled with His courage, His strength, His endurance, and His favor. There is no room for fear when we are obedient and living out faith within the promises of God's ways.

Now if you faithfully obey the LORD your God and are careful to follow all His commands I am giving you today, the LORD your God will put you far above all the nations of the earth.
DEUTERONOMY 28:1

Why do you call Me "Lord, Lord," and don't do the things I say? I will show you what someone is like who comes to Me, hears My words, and acts on them: He is like a man building a house, who dug deep and laid the foundation on the rock. When the flood came, the river crashed against that house and couldn't shake it, because it was well built.
LUKE 6:46–48

How can we be sure that we belong to Him? By looking within ourselves: are we really trying to do what He wants us to?
I JOHN 2:3 TLB

Teach me, Lord, the meaning of Your statutes, and I will always keep them. Help me understand Your instruction, and I will obey it and follow it with all my heart. Help me stay on the path of Your commands, for I take pleasure in it.

PSALM 119:33–35

_____

_____

_____

_____

_____

_____

_____

_____

_____

_____

_____

_____

_____

_____

_____

_____

_____

Lord, sometimes I cringe when I think of the word obey, *yet I am happiest and feel the most confident when I submit to Your leading for my life. Help me to see past the world's hatred of its meaning and look to the empowerment I possess when I receive and live out Your ways.*

HUMBLE OR HUMBLED?

We live in a dog-eat-dog world, don't we? Competition is fierce, and the pace of living is fast. Our society is run by the rich and powerful, and the quickest and loudest. Meekness and humility are characteristics not often found in today's movers and shakers. The thought of living humbly in a hostile mainstream frenzy can be frightening. Yet according to Jesus, it is the humble who are exalted, the meek who are blessed—because these qualities further His kingdom, not ours.

When we're not humble, God has an interesting way of bringing us to such a state—by removing or breaking down what we thought we controlled or by applying enough pressure to show that we never had it in the first place. So we can choose to be humble...or we can be humbled. Trusting Jesus with a humble heart seems far less scary than being humbled in this untrustworthy world.

The humble will inherit the land
and will enjoy abundant prosperity.

PSALM 37:11

Humble yourselves, therefore,
under the mighty hand of God,
so that He may exalt you at the proper time.

I PETER 5:6

All His works are true and His ways are just.
He is able to humble those who walk in pride.

DANIEL 4:37

Humble yourselves before the Lord, and He will exalt you.

JAMES 4:10

Jesus, forgive me for any pride I've carried in my heart, for falsely thinking I am in control of my life. I love You and worship You and give You the glory for the abundance I enjoy and the work I have to do. It all comes from You, and I am truly grateful.

THE 10-PERCENT FEAR

One subject that can quickly trigger fear is that of money—or the letting go of it. Less than a quarter of churchgoers tithe, yet Jesus specifically says to do so. God even challenges believers by saying that when we tithe, He will fill our vats to overflowing (Proverbs 3:9–10), yet most of us don't. Giving 10 percent of our income is frightening when our bills outweigh our paychecks, yet that is the problem...to give anything away means we first must own it, but we don't own our income—it is a gift from God! Tithing is *returning*, or bringing, 10 percent back to the One who provided it in the first place and living on the rest with His blessing. This is the only time in the Bible God says to test Him. Will you?

"Bring the full tenth into the storehouse so that there may be food in my house. Test me in this way," *says the* LORD *of Armies.*
"See if I will not open the floodgates of heaven and pour out a blessing for you without measure."

MALACHI 3:10, EMPHASIS ADDED

Though you are careful to tithe even the smallest part of your income, you completely forget about justice and the love of God. You should tithe, yes, but you should not leave these other things undone.

LUKE 11:42 TLB

You will be enriched in every way for all generosity, which produces thanksgiving to God through us. For the ministry of this service is not only supplying the needs of the saints but is also overflowing in many expressions of thanks to God.

II CORINTHIANS 9:11–12

*For if you give, you will get! Your gift will return to you
in full and overflowing measure, pressed down,
shaken together to make room for more, and running over.
Whatever measure you use to give—large or small—
will be used to measure what is given back to you.*

LUKE 6:38 TLB

_____

_____

_____

_____

_____

_____

_____

_____

_____

_____

_____

*Lord, I am constantly amazed at how far You stretch my dollars when I'm faithful
to tithe. Where I don't see a way, You make a way. When my bills outweigh
my budget, You come through. Every time. I pray for anyone who struggles
with tithing. Let me be a trumpet blast announcing Your faithfulness to every
follower who trusts You in this.*

FAITH IN GIVING

In addition to the fear of bringing our full tithe to the church, there is also the subject of giving *beyond* the tithe. Yes, Jesus says to bring our tithes *and* offerings! This really digs deep into whether or not we believe that God will provide enough to pay all the bills after we give in both ways. The enemy whispers lies and convinces us there won't be enough to cover our own needs, that we'll find more enjoyment spending on ourselves than on others, that what little we may have to give isn't enough anyway. But no matter how much or little is given, when we give with thought, trust, and gratefulness, He sees and sends it back, oftentimes greater than before. Fear of giving is not of God—faith in giving is.

A poor widow came and dropped in two tiny coins worth very little. Summoning His disciples, [Jesus] said to them, "Truly I tell you, this poor widow has put more into the treasury than all the others."

MARK 12:42–43

Each person should do as he has decided in his heart—not reluctantly or out of compulsion, since God loves a cheerful giver.

II CORINTHIANS 9:7

Will a man rob God? Surely not! And yet you have robbed Me. "What do you mean? When did we ever rob You?" You have robbed me of the tithes and offerings due Me.

MALACHI 3:8 TLB

Then the LORD your God will choose a place where He is
to be worshiped. To that place you must bring everything
I tell you: your burnt offerings and sacrifices, your offerings
of a tenth of what you gain, your special gifts,
and all your best things you promised to the LORD.

DEUTERONOMY 12:11 NCV

_____

_____

_____

_____

_____

_____

_____

_____

_____

_____

_____

_____

Lord, I know that giving is a matter of the heart. When I ask, "Will I trust You or not?"
I want my answer to be "yes," but my actions don't always line up. Help me to let go
of the hold I have on my money and view it in its rightful place—in Your hands.
Help me to be a good steward outside the confines of my bank balance.

GOD'S RECIPES FOR FAITH

If you like to cook, you understand the need for recipes. Not just to use as a guide for measuring and preparing, but so you can recreate the same dish with consistent results every time. Plus, when a recipe is written down, you are able to share it with others who want to make that dish for themselves. The Bible is much like a recipe God has shared with us. His recipe for faith is strewn throughout, from Genesis to Revelation. It contains story after story of ordinary people He used in miraculous ways because of their faith—*and* even when their faith wavered. The outcomes are all reliably the same in that God's power and glory were revealed every time. Reading and meditating on God's Word is a fail-safe recipe for a strong and growing faith—enough to stand firm no matter what you are facing.

Remember Your word to Your servant;
You have given me hope through it.

PSALM 119:49

Strengthen me through Your word.
Keep me from the way of deceit
and graciously give me Your instruction.

PSALM 119:28–29

The revelation of Your words brings light
and gives understanding to the inexperienced.

PSALM 119:130

Let the word of Christ dwell richly among you, in all wisdom teaching and admonishing one another through psalms, hymns, and spiritual songs, singing to God with gratitude in your hearts.

COLOSSIANS 3:16

Father, I find such comfort when I read Your Word. It breathes new life deep into my heart. It is rich with guidance and truth, which I so desperately need every day. Thank You for such a great gift filled with blessing and love from Your heart to mine.

FAITH WITHIN THE CHURCH

Even the greatest of spiritual giants go through times that challenge their faith. It seems sometimes that the more faith one has, the more it is tested. This is why it's so very important to lift up one another with encouragement and prayer. When your faith is strong, it can be shared with someone who needs more. And when you are downcast, a fellow believer can do the same for you. Whether a pastor or deacon, a janitor or volunteer, every believer is a coworker in the gospel of Christ. We are called to help, support, and intercede on behalf of one another in action and in prayer. Faith is not to be imparted only outside the church but within its walls as well, seven days a week.

We sent Timothy, our brother and God's coworker in the gospel
of Christ, to strengthen and encourage you concerning your faith,
so that no one will be shaken by these afflictions....
Therefore, brothers and sisters, in all our distress and affliction,
we were encouraged about you through your faith.

I THESSALONIANS 3:2–3, 7

The craftsman encourages the metalworker;
the one who flattens with the hammer encourages the one
who strikes the anvil, saying of the soldering, "It is good."

ISAIAH 41:7

Peter was kept in prison, but the church
was praying fervently to God for him.

ACTS 12:5

*For I [Paul] want very much to see you, so that I may impart
to you some spiritual gift to strengthen you, that is, to be
mutually encouraged by each other's faith, both yours and mine.*

ROMANS 1:11–12

_____

_____

_____

_____

_____

_____

_____

_____

_____

_____

_____

_____

_____

_____

_____

*Lord, give me the mind to reach out more to my brothers and sisters in Christ
through prayer and words of encouragement. Don't let me be so busy that I don't
make time to stop and speak life and faith into someone else who needs it.*

HE CARES, PART ONE

Sometimes life as usual comes to a sudden halt. Through death, tragedy, sickness, loss—normal routines, expectations, and ways of living are gone in an instant. Life will never be the same as it was. Outwardly free-flowing prayers become a silent plea. Thoughts are random and disconnected. It's when one looks harder than ever to see God and asks, "Why? Where are You? What am I to do now?" It's also when He's able to reach into the depths of our hearts we didn't know were there and instill a whole new realm of healing power and loving assurance to undergird and support. It's when Jesus prays on our behalf while carrying us on the stretcher of His loving arms.

We may never know why some things happen, but we can always know Who is with us—to help and to heal, and sometimes just to be. He is our love, and He cares.

In the same way the Spirit [comes to us and] helps us in our weakness.
We do not know what prayer to offer or how to offer it as we should,
but the Spirit Himself [knows our need and at the right time]
intercedes on our behalf with sighs and groanings too deep for words.

ROMANS 8:26 AMP

I consider that the sufferings of this present time
are not worth comparing with the glory
that is going to be revealed to us.

ROMANS 8:18

He who searches our hearts knows the mind of the Spirit,
because He intercedes for the saints according to the will of God.

ROMANS 8:27

Lord, thank You for Your love...for Your tender care...and for Your presence.
Thank You for carrying me when I can no longer stand. Thank You for holding
my life in Your very hands and for Your promise never to leave.

HE CARES, PART TWO

At any given time, each of us knows someone who's been thrust into tragedy. The news of their demise makes our hearts miss a beat and our minds crave a moment of silence to wrap our thoughts around their plight. A natural response might be to rush in to help, but a wall of fear holds us back. We face the fear of not knowing what to do or say, and of experiencing their pain—and who wants to willingly step into pain? Besides, there are safer steps to take. *I'll send a card. I'll call the neighbor to see how she's doing. I'll wait to reach out after his emotions have calmed and he is in more control of the situation.*

But Jesus commands us to bear one another's burdens the way He bears ours—up close, in the middle of the mire. When we do, there is a "knowing" of His presence that causes His pure and holy love to *abound.* Walking toward our neighbor's broken world opens floodgates of His compassion through us. What a gift!

Stoop down and reach out to those who are oppressed.
Share their burdens, and so complete Christ's law.
If you think you are too good for that, you are badly deceived.

GALATIANS 6:2–3 THE MESSAGE

"Which of these three do you think proved to be a neighbor to the man who fell into the hands of the robbers?" "The one who showed mercy to him,"
he said. Then Jesus told him, "Go and do the same."

LUKE 10:36–37

Let us not love in word or speech, but in action and in truth.

I JOHN 3:18

Blessed be the Lord! Day after day He bears our burdens;
God is our salvation.

PSALM 68:19

_____

Lord, I can think of times I stayed at a distance when someone else needed help,
and I'm sorry. I can't go back and redo my actions, but I can change them going
forward. Give me the courage and compassion needed to help ease my neighbor's
pain—the same way You help me. To You be all the glory.

WHEN IN A VALLEY

Anytime we go through a valley of problems and don't see a way out, it's only natural to ask God to change the circumstances. Of course, we don't want to struggle with upheaval and discomforting, painful trials, especially when they drag out over time. But as faithful and loving as God is, He doesn't promise to change our surroundings—He promises to help us through them. His Word says He will lead us and satisfy us in a parched land, and that means He *will*. Sometimes God allows a deep and rugged path to increase our dependence on Him and to grow our faith. Other times hardship must occur for His wonder to shine through. It's during these times we must remember that His ways are not our ways, but we can always trust them to be what's best for us and for His glory.

The LORD will always lead you, satisfy you in a parched land, and strengthen your bones. You will be like a watered garden and like a spring whose water never runs dry.

ISAIAH 58:11

For as the sky soars high above earth, so the way I work surpasses the way you work, and the way I think is beyond the way you think.... So will the words that come out of My mouth not come back empty-handed. They'll do the work I sent them to do, they'll complete the assignment I gave them.

ISAIAH 55:9–11 THE MESSAGE

When I am afraid, I will trust in You.
In God, whose word I praise, in God I trust;
I will not be afraid.

PSALM 56:3-4

Lord, sometimes I don't understand my circumstances and wonder where You are. Help me to hold on to hope. Help me to hold Your Words of truth and love close to my heart. Help me never to stop believing that You are with me, working Your good, even when my eyes can't see.

WAITING IN FAITH, PART ONE

It takes faith to step toward a calling or dream that God has placed on your heart. You plan, work, and press forward not knowing how all the needs will be met, but you know it's what you're supposed to do. You have faith and trust that God knows what He's doing, and that's enough. But there's another kind of faith that can, at times, be even more challenging. It's when you see opportunity and open doors and God says, "Wait."

Waiting—on His timing, on His instruction—can be *excruciating*. Especially when all outward appearances seem to scream for you to move now. But having faith to wait brings gifts of indescribable peace and favor. No matter what people do or say to tempt you to move, there is a greater "knowing" deep down that God gives as He says, "Trust Me." So when He says to wait, wait. And remember He sees the bigger picture and has a greater plan than we are ever capable of understanding. Let that be enough.

Be still before the LORD and wait patiently for him;
fret not yourself over the one who prospers in his way.

PSALM 37:7 ESV

See how the farmer waits for the precious fruit of the earth
and is patient with it until it receives the early and the late rains.

JAMES 5:7

When God made a promise to Abraham, since He had no one greater
to swear by, He swore by Himself: I will indeed bless you,
and I will greatly multiply you. And so, after waiting patiently,
Abraham obtained the promise.

HEBREWS 6:13–15

Wait for the LORD; be strong, and let your heart be courageous.
Wait for the LORD.

PSALM 27:14

Lord, I confess it is hard to wait, especially when circumstances are pointing to the fulfillment of my dreams. I want to be in the center of Your will and experience the blessing that brings. So I will wait. Please give me the patience and discipline to remain still until You say it is time to move.

WAITING IN FAITH, PART TWO

Another circumstance that makes waiting excruciating is when external surroundings are bleak and there doesn't appear to be any hope for change. Someone you love may be sick and the long-term diagnosis isn't good. Or maybe you're the one dealing with a chronic condition, hoping the next treatment will provide relief. Or maybe you've lost your job, and after countless interviews, you still haven't gotten the call saying you're hired. Questions about your ability, even God's faithfulness, can bring on doubt and despair. But take heart—*God is in the waiting*. He is with you, and He cares. He isn't hiding in the shadows watching from a distance. He is working out His bigger plan for your future, orchestrating events and people to help strengthen and carry you into a new day and season.

Now this is what the LORD says... "Do not fear, for I have redeemed you;
I have called you by your name; you are Mine. I will be with you
when you pass through the waters, and when you pass through
the rivers, they will not overwhelm you. You will not be scorched
when you walk through the fire, and the flame will not burn you.
For I am the LORD your God, the Holy One of Israel, and your Savior.

ISAIAH 43:1–3

> *Now if we hope for what we do not see,*
> *we eagerly wait for it with patience.*

ROMANS 8:25

_____

_____

_____

_____

_____

_____

_____

_____

_____

_____

_____

_____

_____

_____

_____

_____

Father, it is so hard to wait patiently without wanting You to change my circumstances. But no matter what, I love You and hold on to the hope that You give. I hold on to the joy that is mine no matter what events swirl around me. You are my song and my shield, and I rest in Your care.

GOD SO LOVED
THROUGH HIS HUMILITY

The baby Jesus' birth in a stable—it's the opposite of how we typically picture the birth of a king. When we think of a king, we think castle on a hill, trumpets, and banners. But if Jesus were born in a royal palace, He'd be inaccessible to almost all of us. Given the power of high social status, we only see royalty from a distance. And God knew this—He knows it now. So Jesus came down—to our level, to a place that was so low, *everyone* would have access. God loves us so much, He brought His Son to our humble state so that we could experience His presence to the extent we could handle. Sometimes that's hard to grasp because we did nothing to deserve such a gift. But He did so because He loves us. It takes faith to believe that, and even more to accept it.

[Mary] gave birth to her firstborn Son, and she wrapped Him tightly in cloth and laid Him in a manger, because there was no guest room available for them.

LUKE 2:7

You have given me the shield of Your salvation; Your right hand upholds me, and Your humility exalts me.

PSALM 18:35

He didn't have an impressive form or majesty that we should look at Him, no appearance that we should desire Him. He was despised and rejected by men, a man of suffering who knew what sickness was.

ISAIAH 53:2-3

The Son of Man did not come to be served, but to serve,
and to give His life as a ransom for many.

MATTHEW 20:28

Father, thank You for sending Your Son. Thank You for sacrificing His place on Your throne even for a short time so I can know Him up close in my day-to-day life. He is my good and faithful Shepherd, and I worship Him.

BE ALL IN

One unfortunate thing that can happen after people accept Christ as their personal Savior is to continue living as usual. There may be a few changes, but deep down, they are content to be saved by His grace, and nothing more. But Jesus says that in order to truly find ourselves—our *real* purpose in this life—we must lose ourselves to Him. *Everything* about us is to be put into His care and direction. This is so hard to do. Fear of losing or letting go of anything causes one to hold on tighter, not loosen their grip. Especially when it's what's familiar and comfortable, not to mention when it's someone we love. But God created each of us for a specific calling designed by Him. And the only way to experience His deep, fulfilling, most meaningful purpose is to let Jesus have total control and to be our lead. The only thing He wants us to hold onto is Him.

Whoever clings to his life shall lose it,
and whoever loses his life shall save it.

LUKE 17:33 TLB

For what will it benefit someone if he gains the whole world
yet loses his life? Or what will anyone give in exchange for his life?

MATTHEW 16:26

Now those who belong to Christ Jesus have crucified the flesh
with its passions and desires. If we live by the Spirit,
let us also keep in step with the Spirit.

GALATIANS 5:24–25

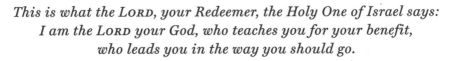

This is what the LORD, your Redeemer, the Holy One of Israel says:
I am the LORD your God, who teaches you for your benefit,
who leads you in the way you should go.

ISAIAH 48:17

_____

_____

_____

_____

_____

_____

_____

_____

_____

_____

_____

_____

_____

_____

Lord, I want You to have my whole life. But sometimes I hold onto parts of it without even realizing it. When I feel fear bubbling up, I can often trace it to something in my grip, and I have to let it go all over again. Help me to begin each day with both palms up, releasing my life to live as You lead.

JOY IN FAITH

It seems that one of the greatest goals in this world is to be happy. One commercial after another shows people dancing because they have a certain product, partying on a luxurious beach without a care, dining and laughing with friends while drinking a new wine... Happiness is not bad, but it is shallow at best. Happiness is conditional and lasts only as long as ideal surroundings remain ideal. But Jesus offers something so much better than happiness, and it can be ours no matter our circumstances: His joy. True joy can be found even when the world around us is falling apart. His joy runs deep into every troubled heart and rushes toward every single cry for His help. It is just one of many gifts He imparts when we walk by faith in His power. He wants to share His joy with those who are His, and He does so with abundance.

Now I [Jesus] am coming to You [Father], and I speak these things
in the world so that they may have My joy completed in them.

JOHN 17:13

As God's ministers, we commend ourselves in everything...
as dying, yet see—we live; as being disciplined, yet not killed;
as grieving, yet always rejoicing.

II CORINTHIANS 6:4, 9–10

I [Paul] am filled with encouragement;
I am overflowing with joy in all our afflictions.

II CORINTHIANS 7:4

Do not grieve, because the joy of the LORD is your strength.

NEHEMIAH 8:10

Lord, this is the day You have made, and I will rejoice and be glad. You are all that is good, and my heart overflows because of Your love and blessings. I am complete in Your joy, and nothing can take it away. Thank You for such a gift.

JESUS IS LIGHT, PART ONE

It is written that Jesus is the light of the world. Have you ever wondered, *Why light? Of all the things God could have chosen to reference His Son, why light?* Could it be because it's the one thing darkness cannot control? After all, darkness has great power. In darkness, secrets dwell. In darkness, crimes are committed. In darkness, thoughts run wild. But even in the lowest, darkest corner or cavern, Jesus speaks. There is no place He won't go. His light demolishes the strongholds of blackness and brings the color of love. The smallest flame brings to life the hope that is needed to end darkness once and for all. It was a bright light in a dark sky that led people to Christ's manger, and it is the light of His love that draws people to God today. Praise God for giving us a light so small and yet so big, the entire world is able to see it and call it our own!

God who said, "Let light shine out of darkness,"
has shone in our hearts to give the light
of the knowledge of God's glory in the face of Jesus Christ.

II CORINTHIANS 4:6

What I tell you in the dark, speak in the light.
What you hear in a whisper, proclaim on the housetops.

MATTHEW 10:27

Look, darkness will cover the earth, and total darkness the peoples;
but the LORD will shine over you, and His glory will appear over you.
Nations will come to your light, and kings to your shining brightness.

ISAIAH 60:2-3

You are a chosen race, a royal priesthood, a holy nation,
a people for His possession, so that you may proclaim the praises
of the One who called you out of darkness into His marvelous light.

I PETER 2:9

_____
_____
_____
_____
_____
_____
_____
_____
_____
_____
_____
_____
_____
_____
_____
_____

Jesus, thank You for the many times You have spoken to me in the dark places
of my heart and lifted me into the light of Your love. Your joy is unspeakable;
I would never have known it if You had not saved me.

JESUS IS LIGHT, PART TWO

Darkness not only has great power, it also carries tremendous weight. Shame, bitterness, unforgiveness—together they can sink a person into the dark depths as fast as an anchor sinks to the bottom of the sea. But our glorious Savior stands with hands extended and says, "Come to Me. Give Me your burden. Let me take it and bring healing to your heart." And when we do, when we give Him our troubles and say, "Yes, please take this from me, Lord," we are lifted to the heights like never before. He replaces our load with His joy—yes, *joy*, even in the midst of turmoil. It is like helium for the heart: nothing can bring it down. What a wonderful Savior He is—a Savior who truly cares.

Come to Me, all of you who are weary and burdened,
and I will give you rest.

MATTHEW 11:28

Humble yourselves, therefore, under the mighty hand of God,
so that He may exalt you at the proper time,
casting all your cares on Him, because He cares about you.

I PETER 5:6–7

I have told you these things so that My joy may be in you
and your joy may be complete.

JOHN 15:11

My yoke is easy and My burden is light.

MATTHEW 11:30

Lord, yes! Please take from me the load I carry. I'm frustrated and tired, and I need Your help. Fill me with Your peace and care so my spirit can truly rest today— starting with this moment. I want Your hand on my life and my heart so I can be free from the burdens that weigh me down.

A CHAMPION LIKE NO OTHER

If there's one thing people like to do, it's root for champion competitors. Take the World Heavyweight Champion, for instance. The winner represents great strength and endurance, and the prize is the honor of a solid gold belt buckle with the WWE emblem engraved on it. It is a coveted prize worn with pride.

It's ironic how the opposite is true of the ultimate Champion of the world. He took on the weight of sin for all generations and, in His humility, wears scars engraved on His hands and feet. He gives us His belt of truth to protect us and remind us that we are the victorious ones when we follow and worship Him. So let us do that today. Let us applaud Him, thank Him, and revere Him for so great a victory and so great a love.

Sing a new song to the LORD, for He has performed wonders;
His right hand and holy arm have won Him victory.

PSALM 98:1

[Thomas] said to them, "If I don't see the mark of the nails
in His hands, put my finger into the mark of the nails,
and put my hand into His side, I will never believe."...
Then [Jesus] said to Thomas, "Put your finger here
and look at My hands. Reach out your hand and put it
into My side. Don't be faithless, but believe."

JOHN 20:25, 27

But thanks be to God, who gives us the victory
through our Lord Jesus Christ!

I CORINTHIANS 15:57

_____

_____

_____

_____

_____

_____

_____

_____

_____

_____

_____

_____

_____

_____

_____

_____

*Jesus, thank You. Thank You for life and for truth. Thank You for the victory
I have over death and that I can look forward to spending eternity with You.
Thank You for so great a love displayed on my behalf. You are the One my heart
cheers for with abandon.*

FEAR DOESN'T STAND A CHANCE

Fear looms. *Always.* The way a vulture circles the sky over its dying prey, fear watches and waits without ceasing, to rush in through the slightest crevice of the mind to devour it. This is why it's so important to begin each day by putting on the armor of God and claiming His protection. Your mind, your heart, your body, your spirit—they're all accessible to harm unless they're protected by the power we have through Jesus. Praise His name, call out to Him, hold firm to the sword—or Word—of God and the shield of faith and wear them proudly! Fear doesn't stand a chance when we stand on holy ground. God has fashioned weapons for us to live boldly and freely. Let us wear them!

Harness the horses; mount the steeds;
take your positions with helmets on!
Polish the lances; put on armor!

JEREMIAH 46:4

Take the helmet of salvation and the sword of the Spirit—
which is the word of God.

EPHESIANS 6:17

The peace of God, which surpasses all understanding,
will guard your hearts and minds in Christ Jesus.

PHILIPPIANS 4:7

You are my shelter and my shield;
I put my hope in Your word.

PSALM 119:114

Father, please watch over me and cover me now. Protect my thoughts from giving in to fear. Guard my heart so that only You have access. Shield my steps from going anywhere outside Your will. Be my shelter for safe passage through this day.

GROW IN FAITH, GROW IN STRENGTH

Faith is a target. It's true. Just imagine waking up and going through each day with a big bull's-eye on your chest. Satan loves target practice, and he will shoot at you regularly, especially when he senses even the slightest hint of weakness through doubt. But don't let that scare you, because faith is also a shield. It's able to withstand the biggest, fastest, hardest arrow shot its way. And, because of God's power, the shield doesn't get weaker with each hit, it gets *stronger*. That's because what Satan uses to try and destroy our faith, God uses to strengthen it by presenting new opportunities to reveal Himself to us. It's His way of growing us in spiritual strength, stature, stamina, and belief. Our shields of faith are meant to be used every day. So let's use them!

You rejoice in this, even though now for a short time, if necessary, you suffer grief in various trials so that the proven character of your faith— more valuable than gold which, though perishable, is refined by fire— may result in praise, glory, and honor at the revelation of Jesus Christ.

I PETER 1:6–7

Our momentary light affliction is producing for us an absolutely incomparable eternal weight of glory.

II CORINTHIANS 4:17

You are being guarded by God's power through faith for a salvation that is ready to be revealed in the last time.

I PETER 1:5

God—He clothes me with strength and makes my way perfect.
He makes my feet like the feet of a deer
and sets me securely on the heights.

PSALM 18:32–33

_____

_____

_____

_____

_____

_____

_____

_____

_____

_____

_____

_____

_____

_____

Lord, I'm holding up my shield of faith now. I wear it in full faith that the strength You provide and the stamina You give will only grow with each challenge I face today. Thank You for such a gift. Thank You for the victory I know is mine because You are with me.

A RIGHT PERCEPTION OF GOD

It's normal human nature that, as we get older, we trust and believe in someone only to the degree we perceive them to be trustworthy. We don't automatically trust; trust has to be earned and proven over and over before it locks in. That's because we've got scars from the times people have lied or been disloyal. In turn, we carry that same mindset into our relationship with God. So if God is perceived as uncaring or incapable, it's impossible to believe in His faithfulness and loving-kindness. That doesn't mean He isn't good and faithful, it just means we don't agree, and that inhibits the level of faith we will have in Him. If we want greater faith, we must have the right perception of God. And a right perception means believing He is who He says He is.

He is Yahweh. He is love. He is worthy. And He is all that is good.

When Jesus came to the region of Caesarea Philippi, He asked His disciples, "Who do people say that the Son of Man is?" They replied, "Some say John the Baptist; others, Elijah; still others, Jeremiah or one of the prophets." "But you," He asked them, "who do you say that I am?" Simon Peter answered, "You are the Messiah, the Son of the living God."

MATTHEW 16:13–16

I [John] looked and heard the voice of many angels.... Their number was countless thousands, plus thousands of thousands. They said with a loud voice, "Worthy is the Lamb who was slaughtered to receive power and riches and wisdom and strength and honor and glory and blessing!"

REVELATION 5:11–12

God replied to Moses, "I AM WHO I AM."

EXODUS 3:14

Father, You are worthy of all my praise. You are worthy of my undying devotion. You are worthy of the glory due Your name. And You are worthy of being seen as all that is good, perfect, and lovely. You are worthy.

FAITH IS YOUR RESPONSIBILITY

From the time we are born, we become responsible for many things. From outward disciplines to inner character development, we must do our part to become sufficient in every aspect of our lives—including our faith. We can ride on the waves of a parent's or friend's faith and live a very inspired life. We might even see God to some degree.

But the *idea* of having faith—or admiring someone else's—doesn't compare to the life-changing realization of having your own. God wants *your* heart and *your* love. He wants to bless you and take you on the most amazing life journey you could imagine. Having your own faith is key to unleashing the power and miracles meant just for you. Having your own faith means an intimate, Spirit-filled life with your Savior and Friend.

Many Samaritans from that town believed in Him because of what the woman said.... Many more believed because of what He said. And they told the woman, "We no longer believe because of what you said, since we have heard for ourselves and know that this really is the Savior of the world."

JOHN 4:39, 41–42

When He entered the house, the blind men approached Him, and Jesus said to them, "Do you believe that I can do this?" They said to Him, "Yes, Lord."

MATTHEW 9:28

Jesus said to [the blind man], "Go, your faith has saved you." Immediately he could see and began to follow Jesus on the road.

MARK 10:52

*The message is near you, in your mouth and in your heart.
This is the message of faith that we proclaim: If you confess
with your mouth, "Jesus is Lord," and believe in your heart
that God raised him from the dead, you will be saved.*

ROMANS 10:8-9

_____
_____
_____
_____
_____
_____
_____
_____
_____
_____
_____
_____
_____
_____
_____
_____

*Lord, I believe! I believe for myself that You are the Son of God, and that You reside
in my heart. Thank You for loving me and for being with me now through eternity.*

BOUND TO JESUS

Faith is being literally bound to Jesus. Have you seen a branch that has been grafted to a tree? A branch from one tree is wrapped and bound to another, and over time, the branch and tree begin to grow together. The branch grows so entwined with the tree that it no longer needs to be wrapped—they literally become one. That's what happens when we place our faith in Christ. There is a spiritual closeness like no other—we become part of His royal priesthood. We are complete. We are forgiven. We are able to walk in His power and experience freedom like never before. Fear no longer has a home when we are one with Jesus. Our residence is bound and fixed where no enemy can be.

I am the true vine, and My Father is the gardener....Just as a branch is unable to produce fruit by itself unless it remains on the vine, neither can you unless you remain in Me. I am the vine; you are the branches. The one who remains in Me and I in him produces much fruit, because you can do nothing without Me.

JOHN 15:1, 4–5

[Jesus] is the Spirit of truth. The world is unable to receive Him because it doesn't see Him or know Him. But you do know Him, because He remains with you and will be in you.

JOHN 14:17

You, however, are not in the flesh, but in the Spirit, if indeed the Spirit of God lives in you.

ROMANS 8:9

Anyone joined to the Lord is one spirit with Him.

I CORINTHIANS 6:17

_____

_____

_____

_____

_____

_____

_____

_____

_____

_____

_____

_____

_____

_____

_____

_____

_____

_____

_____

_____

Lord, having lived with You, I couldn't imagine life without You. You are closer than a friend—You are my very source of life. Thank You for Your promise never to leave.

FAITH IS SACRIFICE

Faith is sacrifice. Putting our plans, our agenda, and our needs into the hands of God requires sacrifice—of self. It means allowing our will to dissolve into His. He has a grand purpose for each of our lives, but He won't *make* us do anything. Isn't it wonderful to serve a God who doesn't dictate what we do?! Our decision to live God's way is the fulfillment of our true purpose in His design. Is it hard to do? Yes! His call is not always easy—it creates complete dependence on Him. Some of the greatest spiritual giants in history struggled at some point or another with this, including Jesus Himself. But the long-term, eternal rewards ultimately outweigh the short-term, worldly pleasure of living for ourselves.

Going a little farther, [Jesus] fell facedown and prayed,
"My Father, if it is possible, let this cup pass from Me.
Yet not as I will, but as You will."

MATTHEW 26:39

By faith Moses, when he had grown up, refused to be called the son
of Pharaoh's daughter and chose to suffer with the people of God
rather than to enjoy the fleeting pleasure of sin. For he considered reproach
for the sake of Christ to be greater wealth than the treasures
of Egypt, since he was looking ahead to the reward.

HEBREWS 11:24–26

He died for all so that those who live should no longer live
for themselves, but for the One who died for them and was raised.

II CORINTHIANS 5:15

I consider my life of no value to myself; my purpose is to finish my course and the ministry I received from the Lord Jesus, to testify to the gospel of God's grace.

ACTS 20:24

_____

_____

_____

_____

_____

_____

_____

_____

_____

_____

_____

_____

_____

_____

_____

Father, releasing my agendas and plans is hard. Self wrestles for first place and wants its own way. Please give me the faith and focus I need for keeping Your will and Your way as my first and top priority. I love You and trust that You know best how to use me for Your bigger, lasting purpose.

FAITH GROWS IN WORKS

Faith is works—*not* to earn anything but to show evidence of our love for the One who saved us. Works are not required; we do them because we *want* to. Doing good deeds and living the way Jesus taught ignites and seals the faith that is within us. How? Faith grows with each outstretched hand offering help to the needy. It grows with every step of service for the community as well as the church body. It grows even mightier when God's presence and power enable us to do far more than we could have imagined. Works are as necessary for a strong faith as salt is for cooking delicious food. There is strength to the body and life to the spirit the instant we take our first step forward in works for God's glory.

What is on your heart to do for Christ? Go and do!

Let us not love in word or speech, but in action and in truth.

I JOHN 3:18

A good person produces good out of the good stored up in his heart.

LUKE 6:45

Conduct yourselves honorably among the Gentiles,
so that when they slander you as evildoers, they will observe
your good works and will glorify God on the day He visits.

I PETER 2:12

Just as the body without the spirit is dead,
so also faith without works is dead.

JAMES 2:26

Lord, today is a new day, and I want to serve You! I love You and want to be used wherever You know there is a need. Show me how and where You want me to help others, and I will go. In faith, I take Your lead and step out of my comfort zone to love a neighbor.

WHAT COLOR ARE YOUR VEINS?

What we feed our minds and bodies affects the level of our faith. A simple way to make this point is by going back to the third grade...and doing the celery stalk experiment. Remember it? If you put a celery stalk in a glass of water with food coloring, within a day it will soak up enough of the color to begin showing in its veins. Within several days the leaves begin taking on the color as well. Likewise, when we are soaked in prayer and reading God's Word, we take Him into our very manner, mood, and attitude. With each heartbeat His Spirit is pumped deeper into our souls, and we reflect His glory.

So, what are you reading and listening to throughout each day? What influence is flowing through your mind and into the veins of your spirit? There's no better color than the color of His love—to fill your heart and for others to see.

Honor His holy name;
let the hearts of those who seek the Lord rejoice.

PSALM 105:3

The Lord is good to those who wait for Him,
to the person who seeks Him.

LAMENTATIONS 3:25

The evil do not understand justice,
but those who seek the Lord understand everything.

PROVERBS 28:5

Young lions lack food and go hungry,
but those who seek the LORD will not lack any good thing.

PSALM 34:10

_____

_____

_____

_____

_____

_____

_____

_____

_____

_____

_____

_____

_____

_____

_____

_____

Jesus, I want Your Holy Spirit to fill me and flow through my very core. Please cleanse me of any negative effects that try to hold my thoughts captive to fear and insecurity. I want Your words, Your grace, and Your love to be the primary influence I put into my mind and my heart.

WE ARE NOT IN CONTROL

Having faith in God means not having to be in control. The ironic thing is, we aren't in control anyway! We may think we are, but in the grander scheme of things, God is over all. So we can either walk in delusion thinking we regulate the courses of our lives (and struggle with fear and doubt every time things don't turn out the way *we* planned), or we can walk in His truth and have peace knowing that whatever outcomes we face, they are in His good and perfect plan. We are right where He wants us to be. So whatever you are facing, rest in knowing you aren't—and don't have to be—in control. Rest in knowing that Jesus is.

He said to [His disciples], "Where is your faith?"
They were fearful and amazed, asking one another, "Who then is this? He
commands even the winds and the waves, and they obey Him!"

LUKE 8:25

"For I know what I have planned for you," says the LORD.
"I have plans to prosper you, not to harm you.
I have plans to give you a future filled with hope."

JEREMIAH 29:11 NET

The LORD is righteous in all His ways
and faithful in all His acts.
The LORD is near all who call out to Him,
all who call out to Him with integrity.

PSALM 145:17–18

Many are the plans in a person's heart,
but it is the LORD's purpose that prevails.

PROVERBS 19:21 NIV

Lord, it seems as though a day doesn't pass that I don't actually think I'm in control of my life. Please help me to do what I can and leave the results up to You. I want to stay out of Your way and have peace in knowing You are working out Your perfect will for me.

LOOKING AT JESUS

Sometimes it's very hard to keep our gaze on God when challenging circumstances vie for our attention. Peter learned this when he stepped out of the boat to walk on the water toward Jesus. Peter literally walked on water—*until he looked at the waves*. It was only then that he began to sink! He took his eyes off the Savior and fixed them on the storm. The good news is, Jesus didn't let him sink. He grabbed Peter's hand and helped him back into the boat to safety. Jesus does the same for us when we focus on Him and not our circumstances. He doesn't always calm the storm around us, but He does take our hand and calm the one within. He gives the power and strength to do what oftentimes seems impossible. Always.

---

*Climbing out of the boat, Peter started walking on the water
and came toward Jesus. But when he saw the strength of the wind,
he was afraid, and beginning to sink he cried out, "Lord, save me!"
Immediately Jesus reached out His hand, caught hold of him,
and said to him, "You of little faith, why did you doubt?"*

MATTHEW 14:29–31

*[Jesus] said to them, "Where is your faith?"
[The disciples] were fearful and amazed, asking one another,
"Who then is this? He commands even the winds
and the waves, and they obey Him!"*

LUKE 8:25

So we do not focus on what is seen, but on what is unseen.
For what is seen is temporary, but what is unseen is eternal.

II CORINTHIANS 4:18

_____
_____
_____
_____
_____
_____
_____
_____
_____
_____
_____
_____
_____
_____
_____
_____

Lord, no matter what happens today, I know that You are aware and in control. Give me the discipline to focus on You and not any circumstance that could cause doubt to enter my thoughts. I only want to see You—the One whose hand is over my life.

OUR HEAVENLY GOAL

Faith is a glorious and eternal goal with a preordained pathway for reaching it. That pathway includes ups and downs, sunlit hills and pitch-dark valleys, but it also includes a hope that burns bright, a hope that won't die. Faith brings the gift of joy and indescribable peace to fill our hearts because we know that we are not alone—Jesus is with us. And when we reach the finish line of our physical life here on earth, we will step into eternity with the Savior. We have an eternal future in His presence. Until that day comes, faith keeps our goal in sight and brightens the way.

Though you have not seen Him, you love Him;
though not seeing Him now, you believe in Him,
and you rejoice with inexpressible and glorious joy,
because you are receiving the goal of your faith,
the salvation of your souls.

I PETER 1:8–9

I [Jesus] will come again and take you to Myself,
so that where I am you may be also.

JOHN 14:3

I love you, LORD, my strength. The LORD is my rock, my fortress,
and my deliverer, my God, my rock where I seek refuge,
my shield and the horn of my salvation, my stronghold.

PSALM 18:1–2

Stephen, full of the Holy Spirit, gazed into heaven.
He saw the glory of God, and Jesus standing
at the right hand of God.

ACTS 7:55

_____
_____
_____
_____
_____
_____
_____
_____
_____
_____
_____
_____
_____
_____
_____

Jesus, thank You for the gift of knowing I have an eternal home with You.
Until my time comes to be with You face to face, please keep my hope burning.
Please shine Your light on my daily path that leads to You.

FAITH ISN'T A MYSTERY

Faith might seem like a dark mystery at times, but it isn't. When we look to God with open trust and dwell on the faithfulness He has shown time and again over thousands of years, it's really quite clear: Faith isn't putting our hope in a random account of miracles and sporadic bursts of power. It is believing in a rock-solid Creator who completes what He starts, and that includes the plans and purposes He has for your life— even when circumstances don't make sense. Any doubt that creeps in is eliminated when we accept His reasons for doing things without always having to understand them (or agree with them). He has been faithful in the past, and He will continue to be faithful—into eternity.

[God] made known to us the mystery of His will,
according to His good pleasure that He purposed in Christ
as a plan for the right time—to bring everything together in Christ,
both things in heaven and things on earth in Him.

EPHESIANS 1:9–10

I [Paul] am sure of this, that He who started a good work in you
will carry it on to completion until the day of Christ Jesus.

PHILIPPIANS 1:6

I want their hearts to be encouraged and joined together in love,
so that they may have all the riches of complete understanding
and have the knowledge of God's mystery—Christ.

COLOSSIANS 2:2

*I have trusted in Your faithful love; my heart will rejoice
in Your deliverance. I will sing to the LORD
because He has treated me generously.*

PSALM 13:5-6

_____

_____

_____

_____

_____

_____

_____

_____

_____

_____

_____

_____

_____

_____

_____

*Father, forgive me for always wanting to know why You do what You do instead of
simply trusting and praising You. When I look back, I can clearly see how Your
mighty hand has been over my life and others'. Help me walk in the safety of Your
care in complete trust, today and for always.*

FAITH IS...PLEASING GOD

Faith is pleasing God. It's pleasing to Him, and it pleases Him. And if there were one thing to hope to accomplish on any given day, it is bringing pleasure to the One who gives us our very life. The way Jesus brought His Father pleasure, our belief is seen, and we, too, are gathered into His arms and loved with an everlasting love. Not that His love is conditional, but that our faith expressed brings intimacy and a depth we wouldn't otherwise know. A heart that seeks after Him receives favor from the delight He shines down, and He is pleased.

Now without faith it is impossible to please God,
since the one who draws near to Him must believe that He exists
and that He rewards those who seek Him.

HEBREWS 11:6

When all the people were baptized, Jesus also was baptized.
As He was praying, heaven opened, and the Holy Spirit descended
on Him in a physical appearance like a dove. And a voice came
from heaven: "You are My beloved Son; with You I am well-pleased."

LUKE 3:21–22

The LORD your God is living among you. He is a mighty Savior.
He will take delight in you with gladness. With His love,
He will calm all your fears. He will rejoice over you with joyful songs.

ZEPHANIAH 3:17 NLT

For by [faith] our ancestors won God's approval.

HEBREWS 11:2

O Father, I do want to please You, because I love You. I know I wouldn't have the joy I hold in my heart if not for You. Your mercy and love are undeniable, and Your saving grace is a blessing beyond compare. I seek Your kingdom today, not my own.

LIVING OUT THE REALITY OF HOPE

Following Christ can bring countless ways to stretch our faith, and those times can be both exciting and scary. They are also telling of just how much we trust our loving God. He gives a dream or vision and we're prompted to go, not knowing where we are going—just that we're supposed to go. Sometimes we know where to go but not how we'll get there. We can create plans and try to put all our ducks in a row, but there will always be missing pieces and unknown parts that cause us to hesitate and doubt. When we doubt, the ultimate questions we are asking are, "Does God really know what He's doing?" and "Will He be in control and powerful enough to provide the pieces that are missing?" Thankfully, the answers are "yes!" And this is certain as well: God rewards our steps of faith. Always.

If you carefully observe every one of these commands I am giving you to follow—to love the LORD your God, walk in all His ways, and remain faithful to Him—the LORD will drive out all these nations before you, and you will drive out nations greater and stronger than you are.

DEUTERONOMY 11:22–23

Mordecai told the messenger to reply to Esther, "Don't think that you will escape the fate of all the Jews because you are in the king's palace. If you keep silent at this time...you and your father's family will be destroyed. Who knows, perhaps you have come to your royal position for such a time as this."

ESTHER 4:13–14

Faith is the reality of what is hoped for,
the proof of what is not seen.
For by it our ancestors won God's approval.

HEBREWS 11:1-2

_____

_____

_____

_____

_____

_____

_____

_____

_____

_____

_____

_____

_____

_____

_____

_____

Father, I am thankful for the stories of faith in Your Word. Abraham, Moses, Esther, Paul… They didn't have all the answers, they simply believed in You and moved forward in faith. Help me to do the same as I live out the hope to which I have been called.

THE COLOR OF CHRIST

Chameleons are a type of lizard that are fascinating to watch, because their bodies change color to match whatever object they are sitting on. Whether a green leaf or a gray rock, they blend in beautifully, as though they are part of the object itself. This is very much the way faith works in our hearts. We can treat others well, live with integrity, and do church, and we'll be like Christ. But when our faith is alive in Him, we become one with Him. We take on God's very colors—our nature becomes part of the person He is. When we allow fear to enter our minds, anxiety grows and changes the backdrop of our color. Even though we're still part of Christ, we no longer blend. This is when sleepless nights occur and poor decisions are made. Pure and simple faith is the only pathway to having beautiful harmony with the holy Savior of the world.

The Son is the radiance of God's glory and the exact expression of His nature, sustaining all things by His powerful word.

HEBREWS 1:3

[Father] I have given them the glory You have given Me, so that they may be one as We are one. I am in them and You are in Me, so that they may be made completely one, that the world may know You have sent Me and have loved them as You have loved Me.

JOHN 17:22–23

If then there is any encouragement in Christ, if any consolation of love, if any fellowship with the Spirit, if any affection and mercy, make my joy complete by thinking the same way, having the same love, united in spirit, intent on one purpose.

PHILIPPIANS 2:1–2

*You will receive power when the Holy Spirit has come on you,
and you will be My witnesses in Jerusalem, in all Judea
and Samaria, and to the end of the earth.*

ACTS 1:8

_Lord, I want to be one with You. I want to live so entwined with Your Spirit,
I will walk in Your nature, Your love, Your power, and Your strength.
I want others to see You in my life, then want You for themselves._

WEAK FAITH, STRONG CHRIST

Time and again in the New Testament, Jesus calls out the fact that we as believers have doubt, with little faith to overcome it. And each mention is a precursor to an example of His power and ability. Does He do this to make us feel inferior or discouraged? No! He does it out of truth and compassion, knowing just how helpless humankind is without a Savior. He wants to provide an accurate contrast between our weakness and His might. Looking to His strength from our lowly perspective puts us, and Him, in our rightful places—not to create a picture of Him lording over us, but to help us understand that He is the one true source of power and strength for us all. Even when our faith is at its greatest, it is still weak compared to the strength He provides. Our weak faith applied to a strong Christ equals victory in all circumstances.

The One who comes from above is above all.
The one who is from the earth is earthly and speaks in earthly terms.
The One who comes from heaven is above all.

JOHN 3:31

When Jesus had finished saying these things, the crowds were astonished at His teaching, because He was teaching them like one who had authority, and not like their scribes.

MATTHEW 7:28–29

Hallelujah! Praise the LORD from the heavens;
praise Him in the heights!

PSALM 148:1

"You are from below," [Jesus] told them, "I am from above.
You are of this world; I am not of this world.

JOHN 8:23

_____

_____

_____

_____

_____

_____

_____

_____

_____

_____

_____

_____

_____

_____

_____

_____

_____

_____

_Lord, I am so needy for Your strength—I cannot do life with any measure
of success without You. I look to You now and draw from the power that is mine
to abolish any doubt or fear that I carry in my heart. I claim the victory that is mine
today as I depend on You._

FAITH IN OUR FALLS

When we are walking closely with God, it seems only natural to have a calm assurance in our faith—the two go hand in hand. But what about the times we stray? What about the times temptation wins and we get so far away from Him, we believe in our heart of hearts we've have gone too far...so far, God would never want us back? Where does the faith we used to have go? Does it just disappear into nothing? Does it dissipate along with God, never to return? The answer is, it's still there. God doesn't leave us—we do the leaving. He's still there, unchanged, holding onto faith on our behalf while waiting and *longing* for our return. God so loves us, even in our sin, He will never leave. He yearns to embrace, to forgive, to celebrate, and to return the faith we left for an even stronger bond of love and devotion. When we are at our lowest, He is at His strongest to woo us back home into His arms.

[The prodigal son] longed to eat his fill from the pods that the pigs were eating, but no one would give him anything. When he came to his senses, he said... "I'll get up, go to my father, and say to him, 'Father, I have sinned against heaven and in your sight. I'm no longer worthy to be called your son.'" ...But while the son was still a long way off, his father saw him and was filled with compassion. He ran, threw his arms around his neck, and kissed him.... The father told his servants, "Quick! Bring out the best robe and put it on him; put a ring on his finger and sandals on his feet. Then bring the fattened calf and slaughter it, and let's celebrate with a feast, because this son of mine was dead and is alive again; he was lost and is found!"

LUKE 15:16–24

There is now no condemnation for those in Christ Jesus.

ROMANS 8:1

God proves his own love for us in that while
we were still sinners, Christ died for us.

ROMANS 5:8

Father, I am so grateful for Your mercy and forgiveness in the times I've strayed.
Thank You for the assurance of Your love and for wiping my slate clean over
and over. You are gracious, and You are good. I am so glad I belong to You
now and for always.

ONE THING THAT IS FREE

Nothing on this earth is free. Some ads might claim you'll get something for free, but sooner or later, down in the fine print, you end up paying for whatever product or promise has been given. This is why it's hard to grasp that the most important thing a person can ever have in life—God's grace—is free. It's free to anyone who believes in Him. What's the catch? Jesus is the catch. He took the eternal consequences for our sins in full measure on Himself. He covered the charge; He bought us with His life. Are we to think He will lose His purchase? No! All who believe and have faith in Him receive grace without measure. There are no returns because of malfunction or brokenness. His grace covers, mends, heals, and rebuilds so that we can be whole in His presence. His grace is the means by which we take one step of faith after another until we see Him face to face.

May you not miss it. May you receive His gift of grace for your life without hesitation!

We have all received grace upon grace from his fullness,
for the law was given through Moses;
grace and truth came through Jesus Christ.

JOHN 1:16–17

He has saved us and called us to a holy life—not because of anything
we have done but because of His own purpose and grace.
This grace was given us in Christ Jesus before the beginning of time.

II TIMOTHY 1:9 NIV

You are saved by grace through faith,
and this is not from yourselves; it is God's gift—
not from works, so that no one can boast.

EPHESIANS 2:8-9

_____

Father, I hear the word free *and sometimes find it hard to grasp the reality of Your grace. It's hard to accept that there's nothing I must do to earn it. Thank You for such a gift. Help me to fully receive it and walk in the freedom grace provides.*

PURE IS BETTER THAN BIG

Jesus said that having faith as small as a mustard seed is all we need to move a mountain. Does this seem as impossible to you as it does to me? How can something so small be so effective? Well, by being pure. Christ latches on to a pure and honest faith, no matter how small it is. And when He does, what little faith we have becomes incredible. The way one drop of nitroglycerin explodes at the slightest impact is like the power Jesus has in faith the size of a dot. But when our faith gets watered down by disbelief and second-guessing, faith loses its power.

Jesus didn't promise to bless a big faith, He promised to bless a pure and sincere one, no matter its size.

The disciples came to Jesus privately and said, "Why could we not cast [the demon] out?" So Jesus said to them, "Because of your unbelief; for assuredly, I say to you, if you have faith as a mustard seed, you will say to this mountain, 'Move from here to there,' and it will move; and nothing will be impossible for you."

MATTHEW 17:19–20 NKJV

Everyone who has this hope fixed on Him purifies himself, just as He is pure.

I JOHN 3:3 NASB

*Who may ascend the mountain of the LORD?...
The one who has clean hands and a pure heart,
who has not appealed to what is false....
He will receive blessing from the LORD,
and righteousness from the God of his salvation.*

PSALM 24:3–5

The goal of our instruction is love that comes from a pure heart,
a good conscience, and a sincere faith.

I TIMOTHY 1:5

_____

_____

_____

_____

_____

_____

_____

_____

_____

_____

_____

_____

_____

_____

_____

_____

_____

Jesus, I want to live in pure and sincere devotion to You today. Please cleanse my heart and clear my mind of any doubt or double-mindedness that exists. I want to be completely and wholly in Your sweet presence.

FIXED ON HIS FAITHFULNESS

How many times have you walked through a neighborhood and seen a cat or dog looking through a window, waiting for its owner to come home? Its eyes are fixed on the horizon looking for the first sign of arrival. Or how about when a child waits for cookies to come out of the oven? He inhales the aroma and fixes his gaze on the treasure he's about to enjoy. This is the same anticipation we have when our faith is alive in a dark and difficult time. We rise each morning and wait and watch for God's light of love to appear. There is a knowing that His favor will reach into our hearts, bringing just what we need to rest in the promise of His presence, knowing that all will be well. Just as the sun rises each morning, His faithful love is on time, every time. Let us keep our gaze on Him.

I wait for the LORD; I wait and put my hope in his word.
I wait for the Lord more than watchmen for the morning....
For there is faithful love with the LORD.

PSALM 130:5–7

Those servants might have to wait until midnight
or later for their master. But they will be happy
when he comes in and finds them still waiting.

LUKE 12:38 ICB

Let us run with endurance the race that lies before us,
keeping our eyes on Jesus, the source and perfecter of our faith.

HEBREWS 12:1-2

Father, in spite of any struggle that comes, I will watch for Your goodness
to shine through. No matter how dark life gets, I will keep watch for the gentle
touches of love and assurance that only You can give.

BELIEVING IS SEEING

You've probably heard, and even said, the phrase "Seeing is believing." We often wait to believe what others tell us until after we've seen it for ourselves. That's because humans often lie and exaggerate in order to get their way, and we don't want to be taken for fools. This was a frustration Jesus dealt with when He walked the earth—and even still to this day. This is because He says, "Believing is seeing." He wants us to first believe that He will fulfill His promises to us. Our faith—our actions on our belief—is what ignites His power in our lives. His death on a cross and resurrected body is the greatest evidence that He does what He says He'll do. He is *the* One who can be trusted in all things, even to the point of death on our behalf.

———

Jesus told [the official], "Unless you people see signs and wonders, you will not believe."... "Go," Jesus told [the official], "your son will live." The man believed what Jesus said to him and departed. While he was still going down, his servants met him saying that his boy was alive.

JOHN 4:48–51, EMPHASIS ADDED

"And many times [the evil spirit] has thrown [my son] into fire or water to destroy him. But if You can do anything, have compassion on us and help us." Jesus said to him, "'If you can'? Everything is possible for the one who believes."

MARK 9:22–23

We walk by faith, not by sight.

II CORINTHIANS 5:7

*He said to her, "Daughter, your faith [your personal trust
and confidence in Me] has restored you to health;
go in peace and be [permanently] healed from your suffering."*

MARK 5:34 AMP

_____

_____

_____

_____

_____

_____

_____

_____

_____

_____

_____

_____

_____

_____

_____

_____

*Jesus, thank You for being the light of truth in a world that offers lies and deceit
at every turn. Thank You for the peace I have in knowing You will do exactly what
You say You will do and that You can be trusted at all times. I hold onto that today.*

GOD'S MASTERPIECE

Many businesses use the power of comparison in order to gain customers. For instance, this model is more beautiful and "together" than you because she has longer lashes and has a degree. He has a gorgeous girlfriend because he has more hair and drives an expensive car. Believing that we are of great worth in God's sight *just the way we are* can be hard with these daily bombardments. Having faith that God sincerely loves us is difficult when we feel inadequate—when we sometimes feel like a mistake. But faith is not a feeling. Faith is believing the right message from a trustworthy messenger—our Creator. God never compares, and He doesn't want us to either. He applauds each and every masterpiece as His own beautiful work of art, because that's what we are.

It was You who created my inward parts; You knit me together in my mother's womb. I will praise You because I have been remarkably and wondrously made. Your works are wondrous, and I know this very well.

PSALM 139:13–14

Not that we dare to classify or compare ourselves with some of those who are commending themselves. But when they measure themselves by one another and compare themselves with one another, they are without understanding.

II CORINTHIANS 10:12 ESV

God proves His own love for us in that
while we were still sinners, Christ died for us.

ROMANS 5:8

_____

_____

_____

_____

_____

_____

_____

_____

_____

_____

_____

_____

_____

_____

_____

_____

_____

_____

_____

Father, I am so glad my value is not dependent on how I feel about myself but on who I am in You. Help me to block out how the world defines me and focus on the worth and love I have in You.

STOP, KNEEL, AND PRAY

If you're like all other human beings, you've experienced some very troublesome and devastating days in your life, maybe even seasons. You might even be living in one right now. It's hard not to give in to panic and then make decisions out of fear—poor decisions, that is. It's these times when faith is what everything boils down to. In a split second, you can either get swept up by the swift current before you and hope not to drown, or you can stop and kneel in firm belief that God is with you and will help. He truly is an ever-present help in trouble, and He has the answers and provision you need—*all* of them. Call to Him. Seek Him with all your heart. He is faithful to those who love Him and believe.

The people began complaining openly before the LORD about hardship.... Then [they] cried out to Moses, and he prayed to the LORD, and the fire died down.

NUMBERS 11:1–2

Then they cried out to the LORD in their trouble, and He brought them out of their distress. He stilled the storm to a whisper, and the waves of the sea were hushed.

PSALM 107:28–29

The disciples came and woke [Jesus] up, saying, "Lord, save us! We're going to die!" He said to them, "Why are you afraid, you of little faith?" Then He got up and rebuked the winds and the sea, and there was a great calm.

MATTHEW 8:25–26

Don't worry about anything, but in everything, through prayer and petition with thanksgiving, present your requests to God.

PHILIPPIANS 4:6

Lord, I bow to You with a humble heart and fall into Your strong arms. Keep my feet firm and my heart strong no matter the turmoil around me. Seal me with Your loving touch and protect me from this storm. In You I place my faith.

POWER IN PROGRESS

Life on this earth can bring some pretty difficult circumstances. Sometimes our own poor decisions bring hardship, but oftentimes hurt and pain are caused by someone else's actions. Having faith in God doesn't make any of us immune to attack, theft, loss, or abandonment. But having faith does make us immune to succumbing to a victim mentality. That's because a victim mentality is not a Jesus mentality. When certain death seemed to be the case for Him, certain life was the actual result. Jesus had the power to resurrect from the grave, and we have that same power in us. Through faith, we have the power to rise up out of the ash heap and keep moving forward. We may not move as quickly for a while, but we can move, one step and one prayer at a time.

God—He clothes me with strength and makes my way perfect.
He makes my feet like the feet of a deer
and sets me securely on the heights.

PSALM 18:32–33

For the joy that lay before him, He endured the cross,
despising the shame, and sat down at the right hand
of the throne of God.

HEBREWS 12:2

I will rejoice and be glad in Your faithful love because You have seen
my affliction. You know the troubles of my soul and have not
handed me over to the enemy. You have set my feet in a spacious place.

PSALM 31:7–8

I will certainly bring health and healing to it and will indeed heal them. I will let them experience the abundance of true peace. I will restore the fortunes of Judah and of Israel and will rebuild them as in former times.

JEREMIAH 33:6–7

_____
_____
_____
_____
_____
_____
_____
_____
_____
_____
_____
_____

Lord, thank You for Your healing grace and love so dear. You help me to rise from the depths and fill me with peace that passes understanding. You bring new life to my spirit and clothe me with Your power. With You, I claim the victory that is mine each and every day.

KNOW GOD

There's a famous quote that says, "If you know your enemy and know yourself, you will never be in peril. If you are ignorant of your enemy and of yourself, you are certain to lose every battle"* (paraphrase). There is a lot of wisdom in this, even though it doesn't include God. For any of us to truly know ourselves, we must know God. He created us. He knows us best. He knows our likes and dislikes, our strengths and our weaknesses—even the number of hairs on our heads. Likewise, to know our enemy, we must know God. Throughout His Word He describes Satan's origin, tactics, track record, and approach—mainly through fear. This means that, in order to truly overcome any fear the enemy haunts us with, we must know God. He is *the* answer for preparing for and winning every battle, every time.

This I know: God is for me.

PSALM 56:9

Yes, God even knows how many hairs you have on your head.

LUKE 12:7 ICB

He is a friend to the upright.

PROVERBS 3:32

Search me, God, and know my heart; test me and know my concerns.
See if there is any offensive way in me; lead me in the everlasting way.

PSALM 139:23–24

*Sun Tzu, *The Art of War*

"Be still, and know that I am God. I will be exalted among the nations, I will be exalted in the earth!"
The LORD of hosts is with us; the God of Jacob is our fortress.

PSALM 46:10–11 ESV

Father, I know the only way to know You more is to spend time in Your Word and in prayer. Just being with You, soaking in Your presence, is a good start for learning more about You, about me, and about the dark forces that daily try to steal my joy and peace. Help me to make more time to spend with You.

BE ON GUARD

If you take any kind of self-defense class, one of the most important things you learn is awareness of your surroundings. Always be aware of where you're going and who's around you. Why? To prevent yourself from walking into a dangerous situation and to identify the quickest escape route. These safety measures hold true to your spiritual safety as well. Are you walking closely with Christ, staying by His side? Are you abiding in His presence? Are your eyes on Him? The greatest defense we have against an enemy that prowls is being aware of his presence and knowing where our true safety lies. Jesus is the One who guards our hearts and keeps us in perfect peace. His shield of faith around us is indestructible.

Be on your guard against false prophets who come to you
in sheep's clothing but inwardly are ravaging wolves.
You'll recognize them by their fruit.

MATTHEW 7:15–16

You, Lord, are a shield around me, my glory,
and the One who lifts up my head. I cry aloud to the Lord,
and He answers me from His holy mountain.

PSALM 3:3–4

The Lord is faithful;
He will strengthen and guard you
from the evil one.

II THESSALONIANS 3:3

*Be on guard for yourselves and for all the flock
of which the Holy Spirit has appointed you as overseers,
to shepherd the church of God.*

ACTS 20:28

Jesus, thank You for being my protector, for being a constant Source of all that is safe and sound, assuring and calm. Help me to be on guard today, both physically and mentally. Help me to take my thoughts captive to Your presence and keep the enemy out. Help me to remain aware of Your presence in my life and to live in the peace that is mine when I abide in You.

FAITH MEANS FAMILY

It is said there is power in numbers, and it's true. Multiple columns holding up a heavy structure are far more effective than one. Four legs on a chair are more stable than three. The same is true for people—we were meant to thrive in community, whether with blood relatives or kindred spirits. When we have fellowship with God, we are strengthened in the spirit—His Spirit—and we are *never* alone. Fellowship with Him and other believers means the gift of encouragement that feeds our faith and strengthens the bonds of God's truth in our lives. We are better able to withstand the trials and remain steadfast in the heat of our battles. Faith doesn't spotlight lone rangers—it welcomes and provides a safe and secure home for every seeking soul. Faith means the comfort of family to do life—*together*.

We are the temple of the living God, as God said:
I will dwell and walk among them, and I will be their God,
and they will be My people.... I will be a Father to you,
and you will be sons and daughters to Me, says the Lord Almighty.

II CORINTHIANS 6:16, 18

[The believers] devoted themselves to the apostles' teaching,
to the fellowship, to the breaking of bread, and to prayer.

ACTS 2:42

*Let us watch out for one another to provoke love and good works,
not neglecting to gather together, as some are in the habit of doing,
but encouraging each other, and all the more
as you see the day approaching.*

HEBREWS 10:24–25

---

*Lord, when I feel weak, I often want to stay home and isolate myself from others.
Help me to speak up and reach out—help me to seek encouragement from others
and know it's okay. Help me not to be ashamed of needing prayer and support
from friends. And help me do the same for others who are feeling downcast.*

HE LISTENS, AND HE CARES

When people meet in a group for the first time, they can often feel awkward about sharing anything too personal. No one knows what topics are safe or how they will be received. Sometimes it helps for the host or leader to have an icebreaker: something to say or do that puts everyone at ease. It is much the same with God—He is a loving icebreaker for us. When we approach Him with a crusty shell around our hearts and struggle to speak honestly about a hurt, pain, or fear, the Host of heaven listens with empathy and instills the warmth of His love. In His presence, we are safe to speak freely—or not. He knows the deep thoughts of our hearts. No amount of toughness can withstand the force of His compassion and the healing it brings. We have a gracious and wonderful God.

I waited patiently for the LORD,
and He turned to me and heard my cry for help.

PSALM 40:1

The LORD is compassionate and merciful,
slow to get angry and filled with unfailing love.

PSALM 103:8 NLT

I will cause all My goodness to pass in front of you,
and I will proclaim the name "the LORD" before you.
I will be gracious to whom I will be gracious,
and I will have compassion on whom I will have compassion.

EXODUS 33:19

> *Lord, hear my prayer. In Your faithfulness listen to my plea, and in Your righteousness answer me.*
>
> PSALM 143:1

Lord, I am grateful I can come to You and lay bare all that is on my heart. Sometimes it's hard to pray—the words don't always flow. But Your warm and patient love remains with a longing to hear and a readiness to comfort. Thank You for being a safe place to be me, just the way I am.

ARE YOU OUT OF YOUR MIND?

"Are you out of your mind?!" That's what we tend to hear when we tell someone we're stepping out in faith to do something against all logic and sound judgment. Sometimes we even say it to ourselves! But stepping out in faith requires just that—moving beyond our scope of sight and into a vision God has given. Doing this *always* brings scoffers and doubters. It will go against reason and require letting go of our otherwise sound reputation. But, ultimately, whose reputation is it? Whom will we please? Jesus sacrificed His life for us, so what is it to sacrifice our reputation if it means furthering God's kingdom and bringing Him glory? So...are you living out of your mind?

I no longer live, but Christ lives in me.
The life I now live in the body, I live by faith in the Son of God,
who loved me and gave Himself for me.

GALATIANS 2:20

By faith Abraham, when he was called, obeyed and set out
for a place that he was going to receive as an inheritance.
He went out, even though he did not know where he was going.

HEBREWS 11:8

[Jesus] said, "Come." And climbing out of the boat,
Peter started walking on the water and came toward Jesus.

MATTHEW 14:29

If we are out of our mind, it is for God.... He died for all
so that those who live should no longer live for themselves,
but for the One who died for them and was raised.

II CORINTHIANS 5:13, 15

Father, I want to live for You. But it's hard when You lead in a direction that defies
logic. I know that living for You means entrusting my life to You, but I confess there
are times I struggle. Help me, Lord, to be obedient to Your call, no matter the cost
or what others think or say. Help keep my eyes focused on You.

WORKING OVERTIME

Have you noticed that when you take steps of faith in a certain area, you're soon bombarded with opposition? Problems jump at you from left field, things break down, people disappoint you... This is when fear sets in and doubt in your ability starts to grow. It's hard not to think, *Did I make a mistake? Why am I having all of these problems and setbacks?* This may seem odd, but it's exactly those times we should start praising God and getting *excited*. The enemy prowls and works overtime when someone threatens his territory. And any time we step out in faith for God's purposes, Satan's throne room sounds an alarm. Harassment is his tactic of choice—he doesn't go down without a fight. It's that simple. So remain firm in your faith. Claim God's peace. Keep pressing on. And keep praising Jesus for what He's about to do!

I [Jesus] have told you these things, so that in Me you have peace. In this world you will have trouble. But take heart! I have overcome the world.

JOHN 16:33 NIV

Resist him [the devil], firm in the faith, knowing that the same kind of sufferings are being experienced by your fellow believers throughout the world. The God of all grace, who called you to His eternal glory in Christ, will Himself restore, establish, strengthen, and support you after you have suffered a little while.

I PETER 5:9–10

My dear children, you come from God and belong to God....
For the Spirit in you is far stronger than anything in the world.

I JOHN 4:4 THE MESSAGE

_____

_____

_____

_____

_____

_____

_____

_____

_____

_____

_____

_____

_____

_____

_____

_____

Lord, I call out to You now and claim the protection and power I have through Your Spirit. Clothe me with Your armor, and go before me to ward off the enemy's attacks. I will praise You in this storm and cling to Your promise to help and to hold my feet on steady ground.

BOTH PALMS UP

If you're trying to live with both palms up—in a state of submission to Christ's leading—it doesn't take long to realize that *keeping* them up can be a slow and challenging process. Fear can set in fast—fear of change, fear of loss, fear of new heights, and fear instilled by the enemy. He doesn't like to lose territory, especially to Jesus. (Remember the spiritual battle that goes on!) Satan lies and tries to convince you that, when you stop a bad habit or change how you've done things in the past, you won't be nearly as fulfilled or safe. But in reality, you'll be gaining newfound peace, joy, faith, and discipline. The rewards don't balance out any loss, they tip the scales. They are *greater*. And by His power that we have in us, we are more than conquerors in every change. Victory is ours to proclaim every time.

Who can bring an accusation against God's elect?
God is the one who justifies.... No, in all these things
we are more than conquerors through Him who loved us.

ROMANS 8:33, 37

Who is the one who conquers the world
but the one who believes that Jesus is the Son of God?

I JOHN 5:5

The LORD is my strength and my song; He has become my salvation.
There are shouts of joy and victory in the tents of the righteous:
"The LORD's right hand performs valiantly!"

PSALM 118:14–15

This is what love for God is: to keep His commands.
And His commands are not a burden, because everyone
who has been born of God conquers the world.
This is the victory that has conquered the world: our faith.

1 JOHN 5:3–4

Lord, thank You for reminding me that Your power within me is sufficient for breaking down strongholds and changing bad habits. Ignite that power within me today so that my faith in Your goodness outshines any fear that tries to stop me.

WHAT? THE WORST CAN BE THE BEST?

Sometimes it's during the worst times we can experience the best times. Does that sound a bit off? If you've lost a friend or loved one and find yourself alone, it's then that God has you all to Himself—and you have Him all to yourself, which can lead to the sweetest fellowship you've ever known. If money is tight and calls for creative ways to expand your budget, there is a greater dependence on God and a new backdrop for His provision to shine through. If life has been harsh and fear about your circumstances has crept in, your faith has a new chance to grow and write a whole new testimony to God's faithfulness. In all cases, His loving-kindness and strength are *always* there to make them the choicest, most memorable times of your life if you let them.

Be satisfied with what you have, for He Himself has said,
I will never leave you or abandon you. Therefore, we may boldly say,
The Lord is my helper; I will not be afraid.

HEBREWS 13:5–6

"Because of the devastation of the needy and the groaning of the poor,
I will now rise up," says the LORD.
"I will provide safety for the one who longs for it."

PSALM 12:5

I am at rest in God alone; my salvation comes from Him.
He alone is my rock and my salvation, my stronghold;
I will never be shaken.

PSALM 62:1–2

Father, help me to remember that hard or fearful times are opportunities to see You, hear You, abide in You, and depend on You more, and that is always a good thing. Help me to rest in You now, entrusting my cares into Your great hands.

THE TREASURE OF FAITH

Sometimes even the stalwarts of faith experience lingering dry seasons that, no matter what direction they turn, tempt them to give up. Give up on dreams, give up on their faith, even give up on God as questions like *Why are You allowing this?!* run on repeat in their tired minds. But faith that endures is like a long, desolate beach with a sand dollar lying on the horizon. The treasure of life and blessing may be small in the distance, but they gleam brightly enough that we need never lose sight. That's because God is there—always. He is a hope that never dies. And as each step we take gets closer to Him, He awaits to renew and restore, envelop and assure. When our faith is weak, His faithfulness is at its greatest. God never gives up on us. Let us never give up on Him.

Therefore, since we have this ministry
because we were shown mercy, we do not give up.

II CORINTHIANS 4:1

The seed in the good ground—these are the ones who,
having heard the word with an honest and good heart,
hold on to it and by enduring, produce fruit.

LUKE 8:15

Therefore we do not give up. Even though our outer person
is being destroyed, our inner person is being renewed day by day.

II CORINTHIANS 4:16

I will always preserve my faithful love for him,
and my covenant with him will endure.

PSALM 89:28

Father, sometimes I do get tired, yet Your light of hope keeps me going.
Your flame of assurance keeps calling to me and helps me to endure. Thank You
for Your promise never to leave me on my own—that You are here now to help me
and to hold me up through another day.

SIMPLE, QUIET DEVOTION

Living in this present day means we have a lot of choices—so many, at times, they can be overwhelming and complicated. Take ordering a cup of coffee, for instance. Instead of ordering a simple cup, we have dozens of ways to choose how we want it prepared. We can get so distracted by the flavor options and levels of milk fat, the coffee flavor gets muted by all the additives.

Trying to spend quiet time with Jesus can be equally distracting. When we read the Bible on our phone, there are pings and rings that interrupt. Reading online brings pop-up ads and incoming mail. But simply sitting in a secluded, quiet place each day with Bible in hand and voice lifted in prayer is the surest way to immerse ourselves in His presence and hear His whisper of love—two things He greatly desires to give. Of all the choices the world has to offer, He wants to be our first choice, with pure and simple devotion.

When you pray, go into your private room, shut your door,
and pray to your Father who is in secret.
And your Father who sees in secret will reward you.

MATTHEW 6:6

When Jesus heard about [John the Baptist's death],
He withdrew from there by boat to a remote place to be alone.

MATTHEW 14:13

Moses took a tent and pitched it outside the camp, at a distance from the
camp; he called it the tent of meeting. Anyone who wanted to consult the
LORD would go to the tent of meeting that was outside the camp.

EXODUS 33:7

Then Jesus came with them to a place called Gethsemane,
and He told the disciples, "Sit here while I go over there and pray."

MATTHEW 26:36

_Lord, I want to escape the noise—I want time without any distractions. I want
to come to the quiet of Your presence and hear Your voice and feel the warmth
of Your embrace. Guard my space, guard my time with You so that nothing
is between us. I want all of me to be with all of You._

FAITH GLOWS

If you spend any amount of time in a doctor's office or a nursing home, the conversation inevitably turns to aches and pains, loss of function, and ailments of one kind or another. Sometimes even discussions of death. And rightfully so—our bodies were not meant to last. They grow sick and worn out over time. But what's so wonderful is, even though our outward bodies are failing, our inner spirits are doing the opposite—they are shining brighter and bolder over time. Renewal of the spirit comes with every step we take that gets us closer to our eternal home. Our spirits grow more brilliant as we keep our eyes on the glory of heaven. No physical affliction on earth that tries to demolish us can dampen the flame of zeal that burns inside, praise be to God. His Spirit not only lives in us, it illuminates our hearts with the hope of eternity—a light that *nothing* can quench.

Therefore we do not give up. Even though our outer person is being destroyed, our inner person is being renewed day by day. For our momentary light affliction is producing for us an absolutely incomparable eternal weight of glory.

II CORINTHIANS 4:16–17

We are always confident and know that while we are at home in the body we are away from the Lord.

II CORINTHIANS 5:6

The law of Yahweh is perfect, reviving life.... The precepts of Yahweh are right, making the heart rejoice. The command of Yahweh is pure, enlightening the eyes.

PSALM 19:7–8 LEB

We all, with unveiled faces, are looking as in a mirror at the glory of the Lord and are being transformed into the same image from glory to glory; this is from the Lord who is the Spirit.

II CORINTHIANS 3:18

_____
_____
_____
_____
_____
_____
_____
_____
_____
_____
_____
_____
_____
_____
_____

Father, getting older is an adjustment, but I'm thankful I get to grow older in grace with You. Thank You for the gift of renewal and hope that not only lives in me but grows stronger every day. Even though my body ages, my spirit is full of Your joy and healing to carry me closer to Your presence for eternity.

WHEN CHRIST IS OUR FUTURE

One of the greatest fears humankind has as a whole is fear of an unknown future. Most of all, our future after we die. We all know that death will come, we just don't know when or how. We wonder, *Will it hurt? Will the process be long and drawn out or instant? If death is the final horizon in life, what is the point of hope?*

The point is, hope derived from faith in Jesus is hope that doesn't die—it lives beyond the grave, just as He did. Jesus' resurrection was proof that He lives—and that He lives in us now to bring us into a final future with Him. Jesus' death enables ours to be a stepping stone rather than an end, so we can hold on to the hope that we'll be forever in His presence. Our last breath here will be our first breath with Him in eternity. We need not fear an unknown future when He is our future.

God loved the world in this way: He gave His one and only Son,
so that everyone who believes in Him will not perish but have eternal life.

JOHN 3:16

[Jesus] will send out His angels with a loud trumpet,
and they will gather His elect from the four winds,
from one end of the sky to the other.

MATTHEW 24:31

Stephen, full of the Holy Spirit, gazed into heaven.
He saw the glory of God, and Jesus standing at the right hand of God.
He said, "Look, I see the heavens opened and the Son of Man
standing at the right hand of God!"

ACTS 7:55–56

You reveal the path of life to me;
in your presence is abundant joy;
at your right hand are eternal pleasures.

PSALM 16:11

_____
_____
_____
_____
_____
_____
_____
_____
_____
_____
_____
_____
_____
_____
_____
_____
_____
_____

Jesus, thank You for the promise of a future with You. Thank You for a hope that doesn't die. Until I step into my heavenly home with You, I hold on to the hope I have with gladness and with joy. Nothing can take it away.

GOD'S LOVE AFTER WE'RE GONE

Planning for our senior "retirement" years up to the time we die can evoke some distressing emotions and questions. Some questions that come up often are, *Who will take care of my estate? Who will care for my family? Who will care for my pets? What will happen to everyone I've poured my heart into my entire life? They are a part of me and I love them.* Of course we can plan ahead for some of those details, but only to a degree. The only One who knows the final answers is God Himself. But there's one thing certain we can all hold close: His love covers. It is greater than the sum of all the unknowns. He was in control before we were born, He will be in control after we leave this earth. Our belief in His faithfulness to our loved ones is an assurance that won't die, even after we are gone. Praise Him!

I, the LORD your God, am a jealous God...
showing faithful love to a thousand generations
of those who love Me and keep My commands.

EXODUS 20:5-6

God said, "This is the sign of the covenant I am making
between Me and you and every living creature with you, a covenant
for all future generations: I have placed My bow in the clouds,
and it will be a sign of the covenant between Me and the earth.

GENESIS 9:12-13

I am the Alpha and the Omega, the first and the last,
the beginning and the end.

REVELATION 22:13

The LORD is good, and His faithful love endures forever;
His faithfulness, through all generations.

PSALM 100:5

Father, I don't know what my family's future holds without me, but I know
that You do. Help me to release them into Your care and not worry, but instead
live with the peace that comes from the love I know You have for them.

REMEMBER WHAT HE HAS DONE

What has God done for you this past week? This past month? Or what about this past year? When was a time He moved in your life that, when you think back on it now, if He hadn't, you would have been in a world of hurt? Perhaps you are in a low state now and He's maneuvering circumstances this very day to lift you out. Take time to remember those moments! God hasn't carried you and opened (or closed) doors just to leave your life to chance. Hold on to your faith in the One who has a plan. He *will* be faithful to complete it in the future, just as He has done in the past.

―――――

Lord my God, You have done many things—
Your wondrous works and Your plans for us;
none can compare with You.

PSALM 40:5

For You have done miraculous things,
plans formed long, long ago,
[fulfilled] with perfect faithfulness.

ISAIAH 25:1 AMP

Seek the Lord and His strength; seek His face always.
Remember the wondrous works He has done, His wonders,
and the judgments He has pronounced.

PSALM 105:4–5

> *I will remember the LORD's works; yes, I will remember*
> *Your ancient wonders. I will reflect on all You have done*
> *and meditate on Your actions.*

PSALM 77:11–12

_____

_____

_____

_____

_____

_____

_____

_____

_____

_____

_____

_____

_____

Lord, it doesn't take long for me to recall the special touches of Your grace this past week, let alone the abundance of blessings over the past year. When I think about all You have done, I don't understand how I could doubt or fear my future when I know my life is in Your hands. You are faithful; therefore I will rest in the assurance that You are with me now.

REMAIN STEADFAST

We all have doubts; we all struggle with unbelief at some point or another in life. Especially when we believed with all our heart that God had led us to a certain place or to do a specific task, only to realize it wasn't what we expected. In times like those it's tempting to second-guess ourselves (and God), run away, and count our losses. But there's something inside that keeps us from giving up. It's knowing deep down there's a bigger picture God is piecing together than just the fulfillment of our immediate calling. Times like these reveal the extent of our faith when it's held under the power and grace of a loving Lord. This is when we need to hold on like never before and remain steadfast.

By faith [Abraham] stayed as a foreigner in the land of promise, living in tents as did Isaac and Jacob, coheirs of the same promise. For he was looking forward to the city that has foundations, whose architect and builder is God.

HEBREWS 11:9–10

God, create a clean heart for me and renew a steadfast spirit within me.

PSALM 51:10

The only condition is that you fully believe the Truth, standing in it steadfast and firm, strong in the Lord, convinced of the Good News that Jesus died for you, and never shifting from trusting Him to save you.

COLOSSIANS 1:23 TLB

*Be steadfast, immovable, always excelling in the Lord's work,
because you know that your labor in the Lord is not in vain.*

I CORINTHIANS 15:58

*Lord, help me stay when You say to stay. Help me go when You say to go.
In any case, give me strength and faith to remain where You want me to be.*

NEVER ALONE

God created us with the innate need to be relational. We are meant to be with others. Our spirits are fed when we relate, converse, share, encourage, serve, and love others. And our very need for relationships triggers the enemy to work overtime by instilling the fear of being alone, especially as one grows older. Families scatter, spouses divorce, and friends pass. It seems that the older people get, the less they are seen in today's society. But regardless of how disconnected today's culture has gotten, Jesus knows and understands the void that loneliness brings. It's why He made it a point to promise He'd be with us always—He will *never* leave. We are never alone. We have a constant companion and friend in Jesus, we just have to call on His name.

I may walk through valleys as dark as death, but I won't be afraid.
You are with me, and your shepherd's rod makes me feel safe.

PSALM 23:4 CEV

Remember, I am with you always, to the end of the age.

MATTHEW 28:20

Even though I am absent in the body,
I am present in spirit.

I CORINTHIANS 5:3

[Jesus] Himself has said,
I will never leave you or abandon you.

HEBREWS 13:5

_____
_____
_____
_____
_____
_____
_____
_____
_____
_____
_____
_____
_____
_____

Lord, thank You for Your presence in my life. Looking back, I can see that You've been with me all along my path. Friends and family members have left and scattered, I've moved a few times, but I know You are with me now and in the days and years ahead. Thank You for being with me always.

HE KNOWS YOU

Did you know there are approximately 7.7 billion people on the earth? That's a lot of personalities for the God of the universe to know, and yet He does—because He created each one of us. It would be easy to feel like just another number in the mix of 7 billion, yet His Word assures us that He knows those who belong to Him. He knows whose hearts are filled with longing and desire for their Creator. He is not a stranger from a distant land—He is near and very personal. He knows you and the problems you face, and He knows the answers to each one. When you call to God, there is no introduction needed. He knows you and keeps you in His care. Let us all rest in that today.

The LORD—His throne is in heaven.
His eyes watch; His gaze examines everyone.

PSALM 11:4

Even the hairs of your head have all been counted.
So don't be afraid.

MATTHEW 10:30–31

Remember, I am with you always,
to the end of the age.

MATTHEW 28:20

God's solid foundation stands firm, having this inscription:
The Lord knows those who are His.

II TIMOTHY 2:19 HCSB

_____

_____

_____

_____

_____

_____

_____

_____

_____

_____

_____

_____

_____

_____

_____

Father, thank You that I can call to You at any time; that I can be in Your presence and know I am not with a stranger. Thank You for knowing my heart and for showing Your love toward me in such abundance. I cling to the strength and comfort I have by being in Your care.

ALWAYS WANTED

We live in a disposable society more than ever. If something doesn't run at full capacity and then some, we don't fix it, we throw it away and get a new one. This includes people. If we don't perform on time, do the workload of two people, or foresee and solve problems before they actually happen, it's natural to wonder if or when we'll be replaced. This is especially true as age and lower stamina set in. It's hard not to fear that we will not be needed or wanted anymore. So it is comforting to know that, in God's eyes, each one of us is loved, cherished, and adored. *Discard* and *replace* are not in His vocabulary. He picks us up when we falter; He helps—even carries—us when we fall short. And He keeps us close at *all* times, not as a condition of our performance, but as His promise in His Word. Rest in knowing you are His to hold close, forever.

He redeems your life from the Pit;
He crowns you with faithful love and compassion.
He satisfies you with good things;
your youth is renewed like the eagle.

PSALM 103:4–5

The LORD your God is among you, a warrior who saves.
He will rejoice over you with gladness. He will be quiet in His love.
He will delight in you with singing.

ZEPHANIAH 3:17

God is faithful; you were called by Him into fellowship with His Son,
Jesus Christ our Lord.

I CORINTHIANS 1:9

*I am sure of this, that He who started a good work in you
will carry it on to completion until the day of Christ Jesus.*

PHILIPPIANS 1:6

*Father, I am so comforted to know I'm not going anywhere that's away from You.
That You will be with me always. That there is a place in Your presence where
I am accepted and loved, just as I am, forever. Thank You for the assurance
this brings!*

TIME TO BE STILL

Today there are more choices than ever for things to do, watch, read, and surf (as in the Web). The challenge is, having so many choices competes with the one that is most important: simply being still. Being still means looking within ourselves and who we are in light of who God wants us to be. And sometimes we avoid being still because we're afraid of what we might see. A ball of dark and painful knots may be fastened in one corner of the heart. In another, pride or unforgiveness may dwell. Whatever we find that is not of God is taking up space where He wants to live, and it's usually ugly to look at.

But God wants to release His cleansing and healing balm in every inch of our being so we can live *free*—so we can be all He wants us to be while living in the lightness of His love. Let us take time to truly look at and release the burdens and fears that dilute His presence and power. He waits this very moment with open arms to remove our cares and fill us with His peace.

Serve [God] wholeheartedly and with a willing mind,
for the LORD searches every heart and understands the intention
of every thought. If you seek Him, He will be found by you.

I CHRONICLES 28:9

Humble yourselves, therefore, under the mighty hand of God,
so that He may exalt you at the proper time,
casting all your cares on Him, because He cares about you.

I PETER 5:6–7

God, see what is in my heart. Know what is there.
Test me. Know what I'm thinking.

PSALM 139:23 NIRV

_____

_____

_____

_____

_____

_____

_____

_____

_____

_____

_____

_____

_____

_____

Father, I come to You now and stop. I humbly bow and seek the places of my heart I have clung to for years, and readily release them to You. I want Your healing; I want Your power and Your grace to fill me, and nothing more. Thank You for not leaving me to myself, but for being my home of love in which to dwell, each and every day.

HIS POWER IS IN US

Have you ever been told by God to do something you didn't feel qualified to do? Peter and John faced this dilemma. They were uneducated and untrained, yet they went out to heal the lame and preach about Christ. At one point they were gathered before Jewish leaders: rulers, elders, scribes, and all the members of the high-priestly family. Talk about intimidating! Peter and John were asked on the spot by what power they were healing and preaching the resurrection of this man called Jesus. And at that moment, "Peter was filled with the Holy Spirit" (Acts 4:8) and spoke with complete authority. If he had relied on his own efforts, there's no telling what would have happened, but he and John understood that their ability came from Jesus alone, and the leaders saw it.

It is the same today: you and I walk by faith in His power that is in us, not in our own strength. In that way, others will see Jesus.

God has chosen what is foolish in the world to shame the wise,
and God has chosen what is weak in the world to shame the strong.
God has chosen what is insignificant and despised in the world—
what is viewed as nothing—to bring to nothing what is viewed
as something, so that no one may boast in His presence.

I CORINTHIANS 1:27–29

Woe to the man who fights with his Creator.
Does the pot argue with its maker?
Does the clay dispute with him who forms it, saying,
"Stop, you're doing it wrong!"...?

ISAIAH 45:9 TLB

*When they observed the boldness of Peter and John
and realized that they were uneducated and untrained men,
they were amazed and recognized that they had been with Jesus.*

ACTS 4:13

---

*Father, the next time I become afraid and start to think I'm not qualified to do
something You have led me to do, please remind me Whose strength and power
I possess—Yours. I am not able, but You are, and I lean into that truth today.*

JESUS, THE PERFECTER OF FAITH

Every day, we all place our faith in something. It can be in our car—that it will start whenever we need it to. It can be in people—that they will do what they have promised to do. It can be in ourselves—that we will achieve whatever we set our minds to. But cars die, people disappoint, and we fall short more times than not. This kind of faith is wobbly and insecure for a heart that needs solid ground in order to live with confidence. But when we place our faith in Jesus—the One whose promises are eternal—our faith is made complete. He is the perfecter of faith that feeds the heart with an everlasting assurance that cannot be broken by anything or anyone.

_____

Keeping our eyes on Jesus, the source and perfecter of our faith.

HEBREWS 12:2

Lord, You are my God; I will exalt You. I will praise Your name, for You have accomplished wonders, plans formed long ago, with perfect faithfulness.

ISAIAH 25:1

We know that the Son of God has come and has given us understanding so that we may know the true One. We are in the true One—that is, in His Son Jesus Christ. He is the true God and eternal life.

I JOHN 5:20

We know, brothers and sisters loved by God, that He has chosen you, because our gospel did not come to you in word only, but also in power, in the Holy Spirit, and with full assurance.

I THESSALONIANS 1:4–5

_____
_____
_____
_____
_____
_____
_____
_____
_____
_____
_____
_____
_____
_____
_____
_____

Jesus, thank You for being the Creator and Sustainer of my life. You complete me in faith, in love, in assurance, and in joy. Knowing You carry me to the finish line of life brings contentment and peace no other source provides.

HIS BLESSED ASSURANCE

Assurance is a heartwarming word. Just the thought of having it brings peace to the spirit like nothing else can. When we have an important assignment, we need assurance we can accomplish it. When we have a health problem, we need assurance we will be healed. When we need money to pay our bills, we need assurance the funds will be there. What quenches this hunger for so much assurance? It is *knowing* God will take care of us. But why is this "knowing" so hard to grasp and hold on to? What brings us to our knees crying out for it day after day? Could it be the fear that the "what ifs" in our mind are true? Or fear that comes when we equate a Godward life with poverty more than with blessing?

Where does God ever say He will not provide? Where does He say we must wait in line because His abilities are limited? Where does He say He isn't willing or able to cover our needs? When we doubt, we are degrading His very character and limiting our ability to receive it. Fearless love is trusting love. And His faithful love *endures forever*. It's a promise.

What we [Paul, Silvanus, and Timothy] told you [the church of the Thessalonians] produced a powerful effect upon you, for the Holy Spirit gave you great and full assurance that what we said was true.

I THESSALONIANS 1:5 TLB

God is not a man, that He might lie, or a son of man, that He might change His mind. Does He speak and not act, or promise and not fulfill?

NUMBERS 23:19

Since we have a great high priest over the house of God,
let us draw near with a true heart in full assurance of faith....
Let us hold on to the confession of our hope without wavering,
since He who promised is faithful.

HEBREWS 10:21-23

_____

_____

_____

_____

_____

_____

_____

_____

_____

_____

_____

_____

_____

_____

Father, I want to trust You so completely I'll not fear but be filled with Your calming
assurance. I want my default mindset to be one of knowing that Your love,
Your grace, and Your provision cover me with abundance, each and every day.
Thank You for Your faithful love.

TO GOD BE THE GLORY

Humans were not made to claim God's glory. Yet so often that's what we do when we take credit for our own achievements—we are actually being grateful to ourselves. We then put faith in ourselves, which is a breeding ground for doubt, because we can't possibly maintain a constant stream of high achievements. But a heart and mind that gives credit to God—its rightful owner—is able to experience the lightness of joy that comes when we are free from the burden to perform or provide. A grateful heart channels the results of our accomplishments to the One who is actually in control. A grateful heart focuses on what He has done, leaving room in our hearts for what He will do. And faith grows.

So let the one who boasts, boast in the Lord.
For it is not the one commending himself who is approved,
but the one the Lord commends.

II CORINTHIANS 10:17–18

King David went in, sat in the LORD's presence, and said, "Who am I, Lord GOD, and what is my house that you have brought me this far?"

2 SAMUEL 7:18

Ascribe to the LORD the glory due his name;
worship the LORD
in the splendor of his holiness.

PSALM 29:2

Give thanks in everything; for this is God's will for you in Christ Jesus.

I THESSALONIANS 5:18

Not to us, Lord, not to us, but to Your name give glory
because of Your faithful love, because of Your truth.

PSALM 115:1

_____
_____
_____
_____
_____
_____
_____
_____
_____
_____
_____
_____
_____
_____

Father, I am grateful for some things, but when I really think about it, there are many things I don't give thanks for. I either take them for granted or take credit for them myself. And I am sorry. Stop me and make me more aware of the details of Your goodness to me throughout each day. I want to give thanks and glory in all things where it's due—in You.

Dear Friend,

This book was prayerfully crafted with you, the reader, in mind—every word, every sentence, every page—was thoughtfully written, designed, and packaged to encourage you...right where you are this very moment. At DaySpring, our vision is to see every person experience the life-changing message of God's love. So, as we worked through rough drafts, design changes, edits, and details, we prayed for you to deeply experience His unfailing love, indescribable peace, and pure joy. It is our sincere hope that through these Truth-filled pages your heart will be blessed, knowing that God cares about you— your desires and disappointments, your challenges and dreams.

He knows. He cares. He loves you unconditionally.

BLESSINGS!
THE DAYSPRING BOOK TEAM

Additional copies of this book and
other DaySpring titles can be purchased
at fine bookstores everywhere.
Order online at <u>dayspring.com</u>
or
by phone at 1-877-751-4347